I0811732

Learning Stories & Teacher Inquiry Groups

Reimagining Teaching & Assessment in Early Childhood Education

Isauro M. Escamilla, Linda R. Kroll,
Daniel R. Meier, & Annie White

National Association for the Education of Young Children
Washington, DC

naeyc®

National Association for the Education of Young Children

1401 H Street NW, Suite 600
Washington, DC 20005
202-232-8777 • 800-424-2460
NAEYC.org

NAEYC Books
Senior Director, Publishing & Content Development
Susan Friedman

Director, Books
Dana Battaglia

Senior Editor
Holly Bohart

Editor
Rossella Procopio

Senior Creative Design Manager
Henrique J. Siblesz

Senior Creative Design Specialist
Gillian Frank

Senior Creative Design Specialist
Charity Coleman

Publishing Business Operations Manager
Francine Markowitz

Through its publications program, the National Association for the Education of Young Children (NAEYC) provides a forum for discussion of major issues and ideas in the early childhood field, with the hope of provoking thought and promoting professional growth. The views expressed or implied in this book are not necessarily those of the Association.

Permissions
NAEYC accepts requests for limited use of our copyrighted material. For permission to reprint, adapt, translate, or otherwise reuse and repurpose content from this publication, review our guidelines at NAEYC.org/resources/permissions.

Photo Credits

Copyright © Getty Images: cover (middle and bottom)

All other photos are courtesy of the authors.

Learning Stories and Teacher Inquiry Groups: Reimagining Teaching and Assessment in Early Childhood Education. Copyright © 2021 by the National Association for the Education of Young Children. All rights reserved. Printed in the United States of America.

Library of Congress Control Number: 2020951549

ISBN: 978-1-938113-91-8

Item: 1154

Contents

Acknowledgments

The authors humbly acknowledge with gratitude the pioneering work of New Zealand early care and education researchers and practitioners who designed and implemented, Te Whāriki, a bicultural/bilingual curriculum (Maori and English), and the Learning Story approach to assessment. The development of the national curriculum was truly an amazing accomplishment and outcome led by Margaret Carr and colleagues (Carr, 2001). Due to the support of the NZ Ministry of Education, innovative leadership and collaboration between Margaret Carr, Helen May, Tilly Reedy, Tamati Reedy, and key stakeholders, they developed the first national early childhood socio-cultural curriculum that centers on a responsive, relationship focused, research- based curriculum and assessment system. It is due to the incredible commitment of the New Zealand early learning education sector that Te Whāriki and Learning Stories is embedded in the hearts and teaching practice of NZ early educators and found its way to the shores of the United States of America.

The authors would also like to acknowledge and especially thank Wendy Lee, Director of the New Zealand Educational Leadership Project (Ltd) (ELP). Wendy Lee has provided unwavering support to the work of advancing Learning Stories in the USA (and around the world) and provided numerous keynote presentations, encouragement, and mentorship to the authors work with Learning Stories. We would like to thank Wendy and the ELP team for their selfless service to the educators, not only in New Zealand and the USA but, on behalf of the teachers across the globe.

In addition, the authors would like to acknowledge and thank the dedication and passionate work of Margie Carter and Deb Curtis who have co-authored numerous books that have inspired and challenged educators in the USA and beyond to be thoughtful change agents, reflective practitioners, to deeply listen and see children, and incorporate equitable and inclusive curriculum and assessment practices in early childhood learning settings. Thank you for inspiring us especially with your books, *The Art of Awareness, Second Edition: How Observation Can Transform Your Teaching* and its final chapter on Learning Stories and the newest addition of *Learning Together with Young Children: A Curriculum Framework for Reflective Teachers.*" Also, thank you Margie for the many years you collaborated with NZ Inspire to lead study abroad trips to help us learn about NZ incredible early care and education system, Te Whāriki curriculum and Learning Stories philosophy and approach towards assessment. Thank you, Margie, for lighting a fire and fanning the flames to help birth Learning Stories in the USA.

The authors would like to thank Tom Drummond for making Learning Stories visible in the USA through his website, full of practical Learning Stories applications for early educators, college professors and students. Always with a clear voice, you articulate with ease the joyful art of writing Learning Stories from the heart. Thank you for pioneering this work virtually and making it accessible to educators near and afar.

The authors would especially like to thank NAEYC and Susan Friedman for supporting the writing and publication of this book, especially for believing in our work with Learning Stories Inquiry groups, and to Dana Battaglia for her editing, patience, and being a reflective partner during our journey writing this book. The authors would like to thank all the amazing educators who contributed and shared their Learning Stories that are included in this book: Cosumnes River College Early Childhood Education Department and Child Development Laboratory Center: Vanessa Gutierrez, Jeannette Mulhern, Eddy Tanimoto, and Lora Wardlaw; Honolulu Community College: Janina Martin and Elizabeth Hartline, Jacob Hau'oli Lorenzo-Elarco, Pua'ena (Chloe) Vierra; KidZCommunity- Stacey Lafayette, Ginger Parks, Kelly Rowe, and Lindsey Shafer; Las Americas Early Education School- Alicia Alvarez, Lauren Boyles, Sahara Gonzalez-Garcia, Penelope Ho, Valerie Hoshino, Mary Lin, Erin Macnabbe, Cynthia Romero, Edwin Serrano, Joanne Yu; Felton Institute's Early Care and Education Program: Azul Muller; Step One School- Laura Barry, Sue Britson, Aaron Calvert, Susana Casher, and Ayla Groom.

We would like to express our deep appreciation to the families who allowed us to make visible the Learning Stories of the following children: Angela, Anissa, Alexandra, Aleksey, Ariana, Carlos, De'Von, Ellie, Francisco (Frankie), Gael, Genesis, Gustavo, Hazel, Jacob, Jazmin, Karen, Keao (Rhythm), Leylanie, Lily, Luna, Nathan, and Thomas.

Finally, thank you to Supporting the Advancement of Learning Stories in America (SALSA) for your commitment to support the authors' work with the Learning Stories Facilitator Inquiry Group and taking leadership roles as champion facilitators of Learning Stories Inquiry groups in your communities. Thank you to all who value this important work, who are open to deepening their practice of Learning Stories, and elevating the powerful, diverse voices of teachers, children, and families.

References

Carr, M. (2001). *Assessment in early childhood settings: Learning Stories*. Thousand Oaks, CA: Sage.

Curtis, D., & Carter, M. (2012). *The art of awareness: How observation can transform your teaching*. Redleaf Press.

Curtis, D., & Carter, M. (2018). *Learning together with young children: A curriculum framework for reflective teachers* (2nd ed.). Redleaf Press.

Drummond, T. (2020, July, 28). *Looking Closely at Children*. Tom Drummond Resources & Writings. https://tomdrummond.com/looking-closely-at-children/writing-learning-stories/

Introduction

Background

The education of young children during their first years of formal schooling creates a powerful social and educational foundation for lifelong social inclusion and academic excellence. Early childhood educators, including teaching assistants, head teachers, and administrators, are critical to creating this foundation along with families and the community. Yet, teachers do not always receive the resources they need for professional growth and development, nor is there a cohesive system for collegial dialogue and collaboration between early childhood educators. Until these issues are addressed, the field will continue to be stymied in its efforts to provide the frequent and high-quality professional support that educators need. This book, *Learning Stories and Teacher Inquiry Groups: Reimagining Teaching and Assessment in Early Childhood Education*, offers a model for better professional support. Its examples highlight educators dedicated to strengthening assessment and instructional practices. The stories and processes on the pages that follow will help educators rethink and redo some of the most persistent patterns and cycles that may have hindered progress in their professional growth.

It is a crucial time for new ideas and new actions, and the field needs a concerted effort by early childhood educators to improve our assessment and instructional approaches and to provide universal access to meaningful social inclusion and academic excellence. This book contributes to this conversation by describing and explaining how to use Learning Stories well in early childhood education, integrated within the professional development process of teacher inquiry, documentation, and reflection. The primary vehicle for this process is the use of regular inquiry group meetings where educators come together and present and reflect upon their documentation and Learning Stories. Inquiry groups make visible the knowledge and insights of early childhood educators, elevate their voices, and provide a forum for sharing and reflecting on that knowledge with peers in a collaborative, democratic structure.

Using Learning Stories

Learning Stories originated in New Zealand (Carr 2001; Carr & Lee 2012, 2019), where educators have shown the value of this approach to make children's learning visible and to highlight key insights and questions about children's play, interactions, languages, cultural traditions, and family and community affiliations and strengths. This book focuses on the role of Learning Stories in promoting new connections between authentic assessment and critical pedagogy in every child's education. Learning Stories can help educators find new avenues toward improving how and why to observe, document, and reflect upon children's learning and development.

The book is intended for early childhood teachers taking courses at the AA, BA, and MA levels, as well as teachers engaged in on-site professional development through professional learning communities, inquiry groups, book clubs, and other forms of professional collaboration and dialogue. It is also intended for administrators, professional development specialists, instructional coaches, and teacher educators who work with teachers to improve assessment, instruction, relationships with families, and collegial team building and collaboration.

The use of Learning Stories is relevant for educators who work in public and independent programs and schools, and who use a mix of varied assessment measures as well as curricular and instructional approaches. The use of Learning Stories can be integrated in both general education settings as well as those serving children with special needs. It is also relevant for educators working with children from a range of cultural and linguistic backgrounds, as well as for programs and schools that feature multilingual instruction. This program is primarily for children from birth through age 8, but it can also work well with school-age children.

Learning Stories and Inquiry

When educators connect Learning Stories with the professional development process of participating in inquiry groups, and with the systematic collection and reflection of material from early childhood settings, the level of discussion and reflection becomes elevated. The power of stories to retell and relive seemingly insignificant moments in children's development takes on new significance and importance when shared with colleagues in a trusting, collegial forum such as the regular use of inquiry groups. The Learning Stories that educators create and share improve the observational and documentation skill set of individual educators and uplift and empower the other participants in the group. When inquiry groups are maintained and nurtured over months and years within and across early childhood settings, a new sense of trust and collaboration takes root and encourages educators to rely on each other's observations and insights to improve their own practice. In a profession that emphasizes teamwork and small group problem solving, there is remarkably little time and professional development space for US early childhood educators to present and give each other feedback on their teaching stories. This book shows how to make that time and space.

Organization of the Book

The book features six chapters, two appendices, and an online study guide. All of the chapters begin with a set of reflection prompts and include additional features such as callout boxes that highlight key ideas, strategies, and additional insights on the Learning Stories. Chapters 2 through 6 feature examples of Learning Stories created and supported by the authors and their colleagues. The Learning Stories are written in English, Spanish, Cantonese, and Hawaiian.

Chapter 1 focuses on defining and explaining the most important forms and functions of inquiry, documentation, and reflection. The chapter explains effective ways to form and run inquiry groups, collect and share data and material on children's learning, and reflect on Learning Stories and other documentation within the collaborative forum of inquiry groups.

Chapter 2 explains the basic structure of Learning Stories and how they can be used for authentic assessment. The chapter discusses the basic principles at the foundation of high-quality, meaningful Learning Stories.

Chapter 3 explains the process for identifying and creating Learning Stories and how to identify a moment or series of moments that might be documented in a Learning Story. The chapter describes effective goals and strategies for collecting material on children's learning, play, and interaction, and the use of writing, audio, and video for creating Learning Stories.

Chapter 4 focuses on the power of Learning Stories to capture and make visible children's social development, play, and language growth. The chapter emphasizes the value of Learning Stories for making visible children's individual, cultural, and multilingual resources and talents for socialization and play on their own and with peers.

Chapter 5 examines how Learning Stories can empower educators to recognize and share children's and families' cultural, social, and linguistic interests and strengths. In keeping with a strengths-based and equity perspective, the chapter shows how selected Learning Stories were created in inquiry groups to help educators reflect on their understanding of languages, cultures, biases, and stereotypes.

Chapter 6 focuses on the role of family outreach and engagement in Learning Stories, and how inquiry groups provide an effective forum for sharing and reflecting on new ways to include and make families visible in early childhood assessment and curriculum.

Appendix A describes an array of assessment tools commonly employed in early childhood education settings, the QRIS, CLASS, DRDP, ERS, ASQ, and PALS, all of which Learning Stories can be used in conjunction, as contextual evidence.

Appendix B includes a list of useful resources, examples of inquiry group meeting protocols, and a study guide for teachers and center directors and other administrators to use this book in their professional development.

Additionally, a Study Guide for individuals and groups is provided as an online resource and can be downloaded at NAEYC.org/learning-stories.

How Learning Stories Appear in the Book

As you read the chapters, you will see many examples of Learning Stories. We show small images of the original Learning Stories, so that you can get a flavor of how unique each story is and can be. Learning Story excerpts are included and discussed, and full text of Learning Stories is also provided.

¿Qué es lo que hay en un nombre?

Isauro M. Escamilla
Febrero 10, 2020

¿Cuál es la historia?

Anna, la semana pasada me preguntaste si sabía que ya puedes escribir tu nombre. Sí, ya lo sabía. Te había visto escribir tu nombre en varias ocasiones. Entonces, también me preguntaste: ¿Sabes lo que significa mi nombre? Honestamente, no lo sabía. Lo admití. Sonreíste y compartiste conmigo lo que sabes sobre tu nombre:

Anna: mi nombre significa paz.
Maestra: ¿Cómo lo sabes?
Anna: Lo sé porque mi mamá me lo dijo, pero no recuerdo exactamente cuándo me lo dijo.
Maestro: Y según tú, ¿qué significa la palabra paz?
Anna: La paz significa ser amable, ser amiga de los demás, jugar con todos, amar a toda la familia y a todos tus compañeros. Además, significa ser amable con todos los demás. ¿Sabes que mi nombre se escribe con dos enes? A, n, n, a. Me gusta mi nombre porque significa paz. Mi mamá se llama Alejandra y cuando llegue a casa le preguntaré qué significa su nombre. Mi nombre suena así, a, a, a. Conozco a otra persona que se llama Ana, con una ene. Bueno, su nombre es Ana María y es la mamá de Allison. Mi mamá y Ana María son hermanas, hermanas de la iglesia. Ana María no es mi tía. Solo tengo un tío que llama Juan.

¿Qué significa esto?

Podría significar que estás muy consciente de quién eres y en quién te estás convirtiendo. El hecho de que tú, Anna, a los cuatro años, definas la palabra paz como un verbo de acción, es muy inspirador. Asocias la paz con ser amable, jugar y amar. Esas tres palabras deberían describir el mundo en el que crecen todos los niños. Como maestros, tenemos la responsabilidad de crear un ambiente escolar tranquilo donde tú y tus compañeros aprendan a ser amables y jugar, y querer y respetarse unos a otros. ¡Tenemos mucho que aprender de ti!

¿Cómo podemos extender tu aprendizaje?

Anna, como una forma de apoyarte para expresar tus ideas más allá de la palabra hablada, te invité a escribir tu nombre y los nombres de los miembros de tu familia. Escribiste *Alejandra*, el nombre de tu mamá; *Ana María*, el nombre de la hermana de tu mamá; *Francisco*, el nombre de tu papá y *Juan*, el nombre de tu tío. Ahora, gracias a ti, ¡sé los nombres de todos en tu familia! Se dice que tenemos familia cercana y parientes lejanos, pero en realidad todos son familia y es todo lo que tenemos, familia. Me alegro mucho que tu mamá haya encontrado una hermana en la mamá de Allison.

Anna, además de escribir los nombres de los miembros de tu familia, también hiciste un dibujo de todos ellos y anotaste sus nombres. ¡Gracias por compartir tu historia, dibujar y escribir! ¿Puedo compartir algo contigo? Yo también tengo un hermano y una hermana. Sus nombres son Antonio y Martha. Nati y Rodrigo son los nombres de mi mamá y mi papá y los quiero mucho.

Comentarios de la señora Alejandra, la madre de Anna:

Encontré el nombre de mi hija en la Biblia. Me gustaba Anna como nombre para mi hija porque significa "Mujer de Paz." Anna también tiene un segundo nombre, que es Ruth y también proviene de la Biblia. Ruth significa "Buena Compañera." Estas son cualidades que vienen con un nombre dado que es de la Biblia. Dios lo bendiga. Gracias.

Getting Started

This book marks a new effort in US early childhood education to link Learning Stories with collaborative and structured teacher inquiry. We, as authors and educators ourselves, consider this book a way of collaborating with you as fellow educators. We encourage readers to contact us for further discussion and dialogue around Learning Stories and inquiry, documentation, and reflection. We look forward to an exchange of ideas and strategies for implementing Learning Stories as linked with the inquiry process to take root in US early childhood education, and to widen the circles of professional collaboration and dialogue.

References

Carr, M. 2001. *Assessment in Early Childhood Settings: Learning Stories*. Thousand Oaks, CA: Sage.

Carr, M., & W. Lee. 2012. *Learning Stories: Constructing Learner Identities in Early Education*. Thousand Oaks, CA: Sage.

Carr, M., & W. Lee. 2019. *Learning Stories in Practice*. Thousand Oaks, CA: Sage.

The Power of Teacher Inquiry Groups: Linking Inquiry, Documentation, and Reflection

1

Defined as practice-based inquiry, teacher inquiry emerges when teachers stumble upon a unique and often troubling matter of concern, something that puzzles and perplexes.

— Renetta Goeson (2014, 3)

Opening Reflections

- What does *teacher inquiry* mean to you?
- Are there elements of your preservice teacher development at the AA, BA, or MA levels that focused on teacher inquiry?
- Have you had direct experience at your teaching site conducting your own teacher inquiry either on your own or with colleagues? If so, how did you benefit personally and professionally from this process?
- Have you considered undertaking elements of teacher inquiry and are curious about what's involved?
- If you were to initiate or join a teacher inquiry group with colleagues at your site or other sites, what resources do you need to get started?

This chapter defines *teacher inquiry*, *reflection*, and *documentation*, and describes the basic goals, structure, and benefits of teacher inquiry groups. In placing a special emphasis on inquiry groups, we highlight how regular, systematic group meetings at early childhood sites provide a collaborative, supportive forum for teachers to present their ongoing inquiry work and Learning Stories. In these meetings, often with the aid of a meeting protocol, teachers receive targeted, supportive feedback from colleagues regarding next steps for inquiry, Learning Stories, and also teaching. In this chapter, we describe and share several actual contexts and examples of teachers starting inquiry groups with colleagues and implementing

Learning Stories. These examples highlight the varied ways that teachers can approach the creation of inquiry groups as well as diverse strategies for integrating Learning Stories.

Creating a Learning Story in the Context of an Inquiry Group

Teaching young children can be an overwhelming, exciting, ever-changing experience that can be the most satisfying profession. Or it can be a profession filled with frustrations, directives, and shortages. Or it can be both. Most importantly, teachers need to feel some control and agency over their teaching and their classrooms or centers, to feel that they know what they are doing and why they are doing it, and to feel in sync with the other teachers (in their classroom or at their school), the children, and the families who make up their learning communities.

When you meet with fellow teachers to reflect on what you each have noticed in your classrooms, to propose questions about what is happening in your classrooms, and to systematically think about what you are doing, you can feel supported in the work you do together and with the children you teach and their families. Meeting together on a regular basis provides the opportunity to reflect collectively on what is occurring in your classrooms, to learn how better to reflect by yourselves, and to challenge one another as critical friends to ask yourselves questions about your classrooms, your students, and their families.

Consider this example of teachers in a preschool classroom. In Room 5, three teachers, Ayla, Aaron, and Laura, work with a group of energetic children ages 3 to 5. They are just beginning to experiment with Learning Stories and to work together as an inquiry group.

Teacher Ayla writes a Learning Story, "Dear Alex," about Alex, a 4-year-old boy learning to write and draw during small group time. Her Learning Story is in the form of a letter to Alex about learning to try new things, particularly in writing and drawing. The story includes a passage about Alex's progression from screaming about not wanting to join the group to being first to come to group time. Alex became more comfortable being in class and working on his writing after the children started using the mantra, "practice makes better," which the children had developed during their group discussion.

After Ayla shares her Learning Story, teachers Aaron and Laura share their own examples of the children's group support for each other's learning. By the end of the discussion, the Room 5 teachers have shared a learning story directed to one child, a learning story directed to a small group of children about making friends, and a video of children thinking about the "middle of a building block" (with several different shapes and middles being shared). In each instance, the teachers share their stories with questions about what the other teachers notice about the children and the teaching practice in the story. We will revisit this classroom and the teachers in this example throughout the chapter as we discuss the process of teacher inquiry with the Learning Story approach.

The Importance of Reflection

Reflection on your practice means that you take the time to think about what has happened in your classroom; to examine artifacts of the work that you have done and that the children have created, including your notes, photographs, audio recordings, and video recordings to jog your memory; and to help you see things that you didn't notice at the time. As you learn to do this in a systematic fashion (e.g., on a regular basis, using tools you become comfortable with, referring to your data to think ahead), you move from reflection to inquiry—to asking questions about what is happening in your classroom in order to teach your students and yourself better.

What about if you teach alone in a family child care center? Can you still collaborate and think together? The more you are NOT alone in your thinking, the more supported and reflective you can feel and be. There are many options for finding thinking partners, even if most of your teaching is done with just one adult and a small group of children. We will be discussing those possibilities here and in future chapters as well. But it is important to remember that there are already reflection partners in your worksites—the children and their families—and it is also possible to reflect with folks who are not with you every day but who share common interests in thinking about this work.

Reflection on what happens in classrooms among children, families, and teachers can lead to questions about the occurrences that puzzle or impress and amaze you. In thinking about these occurrences systematically, you can begin a process of inquiry, which is essentially an informed and systematic extension of a reflection process. In the example, Ayla, Laura, and Aaron are all engaging together in this kind of reflection and inquiry about what children are taking away from their small group teaching practices.

From Reflection to Inquiry

Inquiry can occur via a number of vehicles among teachers such as through examining artifacts (e.g., student work or photos of students' interactions) and through sharing documentation such as observation notes or even video or audio recordings of teaching and children's responses. For example, Ayla, Aaron, Laura, and I (author Linda) watched a video of a teaching moment that prompted Laura to question both her teaching and the children's understanding of the concept she was teaching.

Documentation is key to the inquiry process. Different forms of documentation of classroom interactions and play can be used to spark discussions and the development of more formal inquiry questions. Documentation consists of the many materials that teacher inquirers collect over the course of a project or activity. Through the sharing and discussion of documentation, teachers can move together from discussing general puzzling ideas or specific wonderings about an occurrence to more focused inquiry. Above all, inquiry is a stance or an attitude toward your work. It reflects a curiosity, a passion, and an interest. In taking an inquiry stance you try not to be critical or negative about what you are doing or have done. Asking "what went right?" and "what went wrong?" are not as productive questions as "what happened here?" or "what were the children (or the teachers) thinking about here?"

Forms of Documentation: Provoking Questions and Wonderings

There are two primary forms of documentation: in-progress or "raw" documentation (Meier with Chavez, Eung, & Mancina 2017) and documentation for further inquiry (Forman & Fyfe 2012; Box 1.1).

Participants in an inquiry group learn to experiment with a range of documentation processes and products, and to see how others in the group put their own personal twist or stamp on their documentation. No documentation process or product is ever the same, nor should it be. Effective documentation comes from an organized system for collection of material as well as individual creativity and inventiveness. Effective documentation, though, is influenced by several dimensions. For instance, the preschool teacher inquirer Oscar Chavez, links his documentation to several interrelated dimensions: instruction, children's learning, and family support (Meier with Chavez, Eung, & Mancina 2017, 77).

Examples of in-progress or "raw" documentation

- Photographs of children's actions or constructions
- Children's art products
- Teachers' written observational notes
- Teachers' reflective journal entries
- Brief audio and video clips
- Children's dictations and stories
- Group brainstorms captured as hard or electronic copies

Examples of documentation for further inquiry

- Documentation binder or book
- Documentation panel
- Documentation on the wall or bulletin board
- More detailed video footage
- Classroom or school blog as hard copies or electronic
- Learning Stories as hard or electronic copies

Box 1.1. Two Primary Forms of Documentation

Each inquiry group develops its own toolbox of documentation strategies and materials, and over time group members broaden and deepen their individual and collective expertise in using this toolbox. For instance, the Las Americas inquiry group (consisting of teachers at a public preschool in San Francisco and co-facilitated by authors Isauro and Daniel) has experimented with a range of forms of documentation over the last several years. The inquiry group started out collecting and sharing photographs of children at work and play in and outside of the classroom, as well as the children's learning products, such as their artwork. Participants also wrote notes about what they observed in the classroom and shared these notes in the meetings. Over the next few years, the group organized these materials into books, binders, small and large panels, electronic blogs, slide shows or presentations, audio and video clips, and portfolios. More recently, the group has focused on the creation and sharing of Learning Stories.

KEY IDEA

Documentation

Documentation can include many different kinds of artifacts, including observation notes, photographs, videos, audio recordings, and children's work. It can be unorganized examples or it can be gathered together into a binder or poster for further examination. As Carla Rinaldi explains, "Documentation is interpreted and used for its value as a tool for recalling: that is, as a possibility for reflection" (Project Zero & Reggio Children 2001, 78).

Documentation of classroom interactions, activities, curricula, and children's work can be used both for reflection and for the development of and explication of inquiry questions. To illustrate, we revisit the teachers in Room 5: Laura had begun a cooking unit with the children. As the children learned to cook different kinds of foods and as the unit evolved, Laura began collecting artifacts that reflected some of this learning, such as children's drawings, quotations from the children's discussions and photos of the children and their cooking products. As she examined these artifacts with her fellow teachers, they asked questions of each other about what children were learning from these cooking adventures, including what they were learning about the effects of heat and different kinds of heat on food (e.g., whether things were cooked in the oven or on top of the stove or in the microwave). They were also learning about cooking techniques, such as stirring, mixing, kneading, and measuring. In one instance, children were weighing dough to make breadsticks, then rolling out the dough and finding that both the weighing process and the rolling process were challenging in different ways. Laura was learning these things too! By examining the photographs of her work, the video of one group's experience with weighing the dough, and the children's drawings of what they had done, she had a better idea of what they had taken away from the activity. Presenting these artifacts to her fellow teachers raised new questions.

To include the children in the inquiry process, Laura and her group of children created a documentation panel that was posted at child eye height in the classroom. The panel had photos of children cooking together, cooking products, cooking tools, and children enjoying what they had cooked. It also had some quotations of children's comments about the cooking projects. As the cooking investigations continued, children referred to the panel, reflected on what they already knew, and used the panel to make new suggestions of what to cook, what to include in the cookbook they were creating, and so forth. Thus, inquiry into a particular unit of study pushed the study further and further into the school year and extended *an inquiry stance* to all members of the classroom community. The collection of varied forms of documentation played a key role in Laura's evolving understanding of the children's engagement and learning in the cooking projects.

Goals, Structures, and Benefits of Teacher Inquiry

Teacher inquiry is a systematic, organized process with goals and structures for successful documentation, reflection, and collaboration.

Goals of Teacher Inquiry

The primary goal of teacher inquiry is to support you as the expert on understanding and assessing the teaching and learning in your classroom. By taking an inquiry stance, a position of questioning and researching the classroom, a teacher is able both to be in charge of the classroom and to accept the uncertainties of teaching and learning that occur in the classroom. What do we mean by "the uncertainties" of teaching and learning (McDonald 1992)? No matter how well planned and organized you are, there are always surprises—some are encouraging and some present roadblocks. With an inquiry stance, a stance of wondering about why, what, and how things are the way they are in your classroom or center, these surprises can provide opportunities for learning for teachers, children, and their families.

A second goal of teacher inquiry is to deepen your level of understanding of child development and the role of teaching to facilitate learning. It means to take the position that everything that is happening provides information on what children understand, how teachers understand, and what children and teachers are learning. Having an inquiry stance helps teachers to maintain the attitude that children generally have a good reason for doing what they are doing. Having such a perspective can mean that teachers experience more curiosity and less frustration when confronting puzzling or troubling occurrences (Kroll 2005). Again, in the example presented earlier, Ayla began to understand Alex's resistance to the small group activity as she thought about the challenges he faced with writing and drawing, including how to hold a writing implement, how to tell a story, and how to write his name. Using the phrase "practice makes better" helped all the children in the group to celebrate their developing skills in this area, rather than Alex feeling like he was the only one who was having difficulty.

A third goal of teacher inquiry is to keep the teaching and learning experiences interesting! As you get more skilled at teaching and organizing classrooms, you can become a little bit bored by the routine and expectations—after all, just how interesting can teaching little children toileting and self-care skills be? How can you stay engaged? Through inquiry, even the most mundane and routine tasks can provide an opportunity for investigating the development and learning of your youngsters and your own teaching. In addition, learning about different families' attitudes and beliefs about those self-care routines can broaden your understanding of the different cultural experiences of the children in your care. An inquiry stance opens the teacher to a variety of possibilities and explanations for children's behavior and learning and to different ways to connect with children's families.

A fourth goal of teacher inquiry is to provide documentation that invites children and families to explore together teaching and learning in the classroom or center. The documentation is not just to *show* what has happened, but to *provoke new questions* about what children are learning and how children, families, and teachers can work together to support one another's learning. Documentation can take many forms, including photographs, displays of children's work, stories of children's work and participation, and newsletters, but regardless of format, the purpose of documentation is to provoke questioning and dialogue among all the participants, rather than simply reporting or displaying what has happened (Forman & Fyfe 2012).

KEY IDEA

Four Goals of Teacher Inquiry

1. To support teachers in their teaching and assessment
2. To deepen teachers' conceptual knowledge of child development and teaching
3. To engage teachers with the challenges and joys of working with young children, their families, and colleagues
4. To support the systematic collection and sharing of varied forms of documentation for the purpose of extending inquiry

Structural Supports for Teacher Inquiry

Teacher inquiry groups can be made up of different populations. They can be organized by classroom or family child care center (where there is more than one teacher). They can meet as groups within a school, not necessarily restricted to the same classroom, or all classroom teachers can meet together. They can meet across schools or centers, where teachers from different sites meet to reflect and inquire together. They can even meet online.

However they are organized, inquiry groups need to meet often and regularly, which requires time. Directors need to support this process by providing time for teachers to participate in the inquiry process—time to meet to talk, time to collect and reflect on their data, and time to create and study documentation that can serve for further reflection and inquiry.

Teacher inquiry groups must meet often and regularly for teachers to see inquiry as essential to good practice and as a support for improving their teaching. The inquiry group is the venue for this support and development to occur. By knowing there will be a regular time dedicated to the inquiry process, teachers begin to find themselves thinking about their inquiry questions and documentation throughout their teaching day. Knowing there will be time to note down what they are thinking about, and collect and consider artifacts, teachers will begin to anticipate the process, and inquiry will become more fruitful and systematic.

KEY IDEA

What Is Needed for Teacher Inquiry Groups?

1. Must have consistent membership
2. Must meet regularly
3. Must have consistent structures (e.g., agendas, protocols for sharing)
4. Must have a dedicated time and place to meet

Teacher inquiry groups benefit from an established structure, which can include a regular meeting agenda that teachers can anticipate and plan for. The inquiry group should decide on goals and ways of interacting for their members. These decisions work best if they are made collaboratively, even if there is an identified facilitator or leader of the group.

When an inquiry meeting is led by a facilitator, the facilitator can develop the meeting agenda in communication with whoever is presenting their inquiry and documentation that day. He or she can also act as a timekeeper, making sure that the agenda is adhered to in an equitable and supportive way for both the presenter and the other participants. The role of facilitator can be held by one person or can rotate, depending on the desire of the group and the nature of the inquiry process for that particular group.

It can also be helpful for inquiry groups to follow a protocol when they meet. The protocol can provide a known and anticipated structure for the meeting, thus giving the inquiry group a sense of what to expect and how things might go. There are many examples of such protocols (Abramson 2008; Given et al. 2010), which usually include an agreed-upon structure for the agenda where the focus of the meeting can be one person's or classroom's documentation and inquiry, or the focus can be a particular question that all participants have considered, or it can be a response to a reading that everyone has done. Often the protocol will include time for a presenter to share their inquiry focus and documentation, and then time for the rest of the group to respond by asking questions and commenting on what the presenter has shared. (It is important here to make sure that the focus remains on the inquiry question and the focus of the presenter, rather than on what this material might remind the other participants of in their own practice.) Finally, the protocol can include recommendations or reflections on next steps for the presenter, further questions for this particular inquiry, and time for others to brainstorm their own inquiry projects.

In the case of responding to shared readings in an inquiry group, an agreed-upon protocol can help to focus the discussion and give everyone an equitable opportunity to share their reactions to the readings. Readings for inquiry groups should be carefully chosen to support the inquiry questions that the teachers have expressed, and reading discussions should be used both to clarify and expand on the readings and to inform the inquiry that the teachers are conducting.

KEY IDEA

Meeting Structure for Las Americas Inquiry Group

- Monthly meeting for approximately 90 minutes (supervisor, teachers, assistant teachers, coaches, visitors)
- Group facilitators (agenda, note taker, reading protocol, discussion)
- Snacks provided
- Agenda and announcements (5 minutes)
- Review of last meeting's notes regarding next steps for inquiry, documentation, and teaching (5–10 minutes)
- Discussion of current readings using Text Rendering Experience protocol (20–30 minutes)
- Presentation of documentation and teaching by classroom and by individual teachers and coaches (45–60 minutes)
- Feedback and next steps for inquiry, documentation, and teaching (10 minutes)
- Closure and next meeting plans (5 minutes)

Benefits of Inquiry Groups

As you will see, the benefits of inquiry for teachers and their students and school or center communities are great. Inquiry can provide support for teachers to question and reflect on their practice and to regard their practice as ever developing and as always interesting and challenging. Collaborative teacher inquiry builds strong communities of teachers, giving support and acknowledgment to the expertise of teachers themselves, providing them with a context for sharing the brilliant work that they do daily, as well as a forum for being able to ask questions and acknowledge their ongoing search for understanding of their children, families, and classrooms. Inquiry groups are successful when teachers find them both supportive and provocative.

The purpose of the inquiry group is to provide feedback and an arena for co-reflection and debate. Feedback can come from one another, from a facilitator, or both. Feedback can be supportive and constructive, but it can also challenge assumptions and things that have not been questioned before. The combination of self-reflection and feedback from trusted colleagues can support teachers' ability and willingness to question their practice on a regular basis, to consider change and wonderings as supportive of and evidence of good practice. Feedback can help teachers to realize that they are in this profession together, with the children and their families, rather than on their own with the door closed.

Inquiry Groups as Professional Development

When you join with colleagues to form an inquiry group, you start a new journey of professional development by linking inquiry, documentation, and reflection. A powerful impetus for this collaborative work comes from the New Zealand educator Brenda Souter's sage advice—"Always be open to the world." Participation in an inquiry group starts when you realize that you want something more for yourself as an educator—to expand your role as a transformative educator who makes a difference for children, families, communities, and for yourself.

Collaboration and Trust: Relying on the Group

Collaboration and trust are at the foundation for effective and satisfying inquiry groups in early childhood education. Since all members have their own developmental trajectories as professionals and as adult learners, participation in an inquiry group supports teachers both personally and professionally as they learn and grow. A well-structured and well-facilitated inquiry group provides an ongoing forum for sharing inquiry, documentation, and reflection within a supportive, trusting, and yet challenging community of colleagues.

Adult learners learn best when they feel comfortable socially, have sufficient emotional and political support to speak up in a group, and know that their ideas and feelings are validated and taken seriously. They also learn and grow when their identities, self-images, and roles are supported and appreciated both for their uniqueness and for their contributions to improving the collective work of the group. When you participate in inquiry groups over a long period of time, you learn to trust the process, each other, and, most importantly, yourself. This often leads to a letting go of your fears of potential rejection or exclusion from others in a group and letting go of your fears of failure or lack of knowledge or competency. Over time, as the inquiry group becomes less a collection of individuals and more a collaborative group, participants give over their personal agendas and fears to the strength of the group. In this sense, inquiry groups become a balanced source of individual and communal support for the group, a dual benefit not usually provided by traditional forms of early childhood professional development or staff meetings.

Dialogue and Engagement: Effective Strategies

Dialogue and engagement build trust and collaboration in inquiry groups. When you undertake the process of inquiry, documentation, and reflection alone, you are on your own as you wrestle with such questions as: What material should I collect and how? What is the meaning and value of the material that I have collected? How can I use the material I collected to improve my teaching and the children's learning? Whom can I share my inquiry and document with so I can reflect more deeply? While this solo inquiry process can be valuable, it can also be lonely, and you miss out on feedback and advice from other teacher inquirers. This is where participation in an inquiry group, whether at your site or in conjunction with others at other sites, becomes so valuable: collaborative inquiry provides regular meetings and communication with inquiry colleagues for examining documentation and brainstorming next steps for inquiry and teaching (Henderson et al. 2012; Kroll & Meier 2017; Stribling 2017). It can also encourage group members to stay engaged with the inquiry process when feeling discouraged or lost with observation, documentation, and reflection.

Participation in an inquiry group also enables the sharing of group members' inquiry questions, puzzles, and wonderings with colleagues, families, and outside community members. And as an inquiry group grows and evolves over time, group members learn how to share their inquiry material, take on supportive and collaborative roles, and offer each other helpful next steps for inquiry, documentation, and reflection. Further, as teacher inquirers present early drafts of documentation such as photographs and artifacts that might eventually make their way into a final, polished Learning Story, group members can offer suggestions about the strength of the documentation and ideas for next steps for inquiry and reflection. In this process of "putting yourself out there," group members learn to take risks in sharing material that might reflect on their teaching and inquiry skills and knowledge. There can be feelings of nervousness and possibly even some level of fear, so the group meeting facilitator(s), structure, agenda, and protocol provide structured support for sharing and comment.

For example, over the several years that the Las Americas inquiry group has met, group participants learned to trust their own feelings and the expressions of solidarity and collaboration as the group repeatedly engaged in fruitful dialogue and perspective-taking. A critical aspect of this process involves the language and the method of communicating used by group members (Escamilla & Meier 2017):

- Reading out loud a Learning Story for the group to hear (emphasizing the sense of authorship of the creator of the Learning Story and making the reading a communal listening experience)
- Multilingualism (such as writing a Learning Story in the first language of a child and teacher and providing multilingual translation so that other group members can understand documentation)
- Overtures for equitable turn taking (allowing and even encouraging others to take the floor: "_______, can you please share about those great photographs you've been taking?")
- Expansions (comments that expand and extend others' ideas and observations: "I wonder if you want to ask the children to reflect on those photographs?")

- Complementary moves (statements that indicate that others are also using a similar inquiry strategy: "This reminds me of the way that you use those sticky notes to write down what the children are wondering about")
- Language of solidarity (affirmations of collaboration and trust: "I'm still in the learning process of understanding what Learning Stories are and what they can do for us")

KEY IDEA

Using the Text Rendering Experience as a Group Strategy

- Purpose: To collaboratively construct meaning, clarify, and expand our thinking about a text or document
- Roles: A facilitator to guide the process and a scribe to track the phrases and words that are shared
- Setup: Take a few moments to review the document and mark the sentence, the phrase, and the word that you think is particularly important for our work.
- 6 Steps or Rounds:
    1. Each person shares a *sentence* from the document that they think is particularly significant. The scribe records each sentence.
    2. Each person shares a *phrase* that they think is particularly significant. The scribe records each phrase.
    3. Each person shares a *word* that they think is particularly significant. The scribe records each word.
    4. The group discusses what they heard and what it says about the document.
    5. The group shares the words that emerged in any insights about the document.
    6. The group debriefs the Text Rendering Experience. (NSRF, n.d.)

These specific strategies and elements were never overtly specified or discussed in the group but rather appeared organically over time. Each inquiry group has its own process for identity formation and development based upon each person's individual ways of using their languages.

An Intellectual Environment: Sharing Readings

Inquiry groups are also sites for intellectual stimulation when groups commit to the reading of articles or books that interest the group. The Las Americas inquiry group has routinely read one to two books per year as part of its collaborative inquiry work. The group chooses the readings early in the year, reads a chapter or a reasonable number of pages each month, and then discusses the readings at their monthly inquiry group meetings. For example, the group recently read *Children's Lively Minds: Schema Theory Made Visible* (Curtis & Jaboneta 2019), and these authors joined the inquiry group meeting through an electronic platform to discuss their book.

Over the last few years, the group has successfully used the Text Rendering Experience (NSRF, n.d.), which Penelope Ho, a dual language coach, introduced to the group. The protocol asks participants to select a word, phrase, and sentence that intrigues them. This protocol helps participants to find bite-size pieces of the readings that resonate with the group's documentation and Learning Stories.

As with all protocols, it is valuable to take a flexible approach, and the inquiry group has made certain changes to the Text Rendering Experience. For instance, Penelope acts as both the facilitator and the scribe during the protocol process, which saves time and also provides more flow for her to guide the group through at each meeting. Penelope also types the participants' responses through the first three rounds, and sometimes shows the responses on a screen for easy group viewing.

Chapter Summary

In this chapter, we discussed key ideas and strategies for linking inquiry, reflection, and documentation as a foundation for the remaining chapters on Learning Stories. The regular, sustained use of inquiry and reflection groups is an important avenue for educators (teachers, assistant teachers, coaches, mentors, and administrators) to come together and present documentation in a collaborative, trusting environment. These inquiry groups promote new levels of dialogue, cooperation, and collaboration that deepen the documentation process and support educators' individual and collective understanding and implementation of high-quality documentation and reflection. In the next chapter, we describe and discuss how Learning Stories are a powerful form of documentation and authentic assessment.

Key Points

› The less you are alone in your thinking, the more supported and reflective you can feel and be.

› Inquiry is a stance or an attitude toward one's work. It reflects a curiosity, a passion, and an interest. In taking an inquiry stance, you try not to be critical or negative about what you are doing or have done.

› Since all educators have their own developmental trajectories as professionals and as adult learners, participation in an inquiry group supports both personal and professional learning and growth.

› Educators also learn and grow when their identities, self-images, and roles are supported and appreciated both for their uniqueness and for their contributions to improving the collective work of the group.

› Inquiry groups are a balanced source of individual and communal support for the group, a dual benefit not usually provided by traditional forms of early childhood professional development or staff meetings.

References

Abramson, S. 2008. "Co-Inquiry: Documentation, Communication, Action." *Voices of Practitioners* 3 (2): 1–10.

Curtis, D., & N. Jaboneta. 2019. *Children's Lively Minds: Schema Theory Made Visible*. St. Paul, MN: Redleaf Press.

Escamilla, I.M., & D.R. Meier. 2017. "The Promise of Teacher Inquiry and Reflection: Early Childhood Teachers as Change Agents." *Studying Teacher Education* 14 (1): 1–19.

Forman, G. & B. Fyfe. 2012. "Negotiated Learning Through Design, Documentation, and Discourse." In *The Hundred Languages of Children: The Reggio Emilia Experience in Transformation*, eds. C. Edwards, L. Gandini, & G. Forman, 3rd ed., 247–272. Santa Barbara, CA: Praeger.

Given, H., L. Kuh, D. LeeKeenan, B. Mardell, S. Redditt, & S. Twombly. 2010. "Changing School Culture: Using Documentation to Support Collaborative Inquiry." *Theory Into Practice* 49: 36–46.

Goeson, R. 2014. "Finding Our Voices Through Narrative Inquiry: Exploring a Conflict of Cultures." *Voices of Practitioners* 9 (1): 1–22.

Henderson, B., D. Meier, G. Perry, & A.J. Stremmel. 2012. "The Nature of Teacher Research." *Voices of Practitioners*: 1–7.

Kroll, L.R. 2005. "Making Inquiry a Habit of Mind: Learning to Use Inquiry to Understand and Improve Practice." *Studying Teacher Education* 1 (2): 179–193.

Kroll, L.R., & D.R. Meier. 2017. *Documentation and Inquiry in the Early Childhood Classroom: Research Stories from Urban Centers and Schools*. New York: Routledge.

McDonald, J.P. 1992. *Teaching: Making Sense of an Uncertain Craft*. New York: Teachers College Press.

Meier, D.R. With O. Chavez, L.L. Eung, & J. Mancina. 2017. "Zaida T. Rodriguez Early Education School: Telling a Story on the Walls." In Documentation and Inquiry in the Early Childhood Classroom. L.R. Kroll & D.R. Meier, 74–90. New York: Routledge.

NSRF (National School Reform Faculty). n.d. "Text Rendering Experience." Bloomington, IN: NSRF. www.nsrfharmony.org/wp-content/uploads/2017/10/text_rendering_0.pdf.

Project Zero & Reggio Children. 2001. *Making Learning Visible: Children as Individual and Group Learners*. Cambridge, MA: Reggio Children & Project Zero.

Stribling, S.M. 2017. "The Transformative Power of Action Research." In *Experiments in Agency: New Research—New Voices*, eds. S.F. Baily, F. Shahrokhi, & T. Carsillo, 27–38. Rotterdam, Netherlands: Sense Publishers.

2

Learning Stories as an Approach and Framework for Authentic Assessment and Critical Pedagogy

Stories have the power to explore people's relationships, both public and private, with their environment and with one another. In this way, stories illuminate knowledge in such a way that it connects to the roots of who we are as individuals and as a community.

— Maenette K.P. Benham (2007, 513)

Opening Reflections

- What does telling a story mean to you?
- How have you used story writing and storytelling in your classroom?
- How have children responded to different kinds of stories?
- If you have had experience with Learning Stories, what are the benefits of it as an approach and framework that promotes authentic assessment and critical pedagogy?
- If you are new to Learning Stories, what are you curious about and what are your questions?

Learning Stories is a narrative-based approach to assessment and teaching created by educators in New Zealand to highlight children's strengths and improve instruction based on the interests, talents, needs, and rights of children and their families (Carr 2001; Carr & Lee 2012, 2019). In the last decade, a number of US early childhood educators have explored innovative ideas to document children's learning through narrative assessment approaches (Carter 2017; Meier & Stremmel 2010; White 2017), breaking away from more traditional methods which view children and families from a deficit perspective, highlighting what they cannot do instead of what they can.

Learning Stories are formative assessments that offer the possibility of re-imagining children as competent learners and teachers as critical thinkers, advocates, creative writers, and genuinely invested in their work. In this chapter, we borrow foundational ideas of the New Zealand approach to explain the goals, elements, and benefits of Learning Stories for US early childhood teachers and how Learning Stories can help link authentic assessment with critical pedagogy.

Learning Stories provide a framework for teachers to observe children naturally in their learning environments and to observe and document children's personal interests, discoveries, and talents. Learning Stories are told by educators from a strength-based perspective, viewing the whole child as a person rather than fragmenting the child into separate parts based on predetermined assessment measures. The Learning Stories framework honors multiple perspectives to create more complete images of the learners, including the voices of teachers as narrators, the voices and actions of children as active participants in the learning process, and the voices of families who offer their perspective as the most important teachers in their children's lives.

Whether teachers are in private, independent, or public early childhood contexts, the Learning Stories approach is an effective way for them to observe and document small moments of learning and growth in young children with specific examples of children's questions, puzzles, and discoveries. The approach also allows teachers to document and share their own learning as critical observers, storytellers, writers, and colleagues. For teachers and leaders working in sites that utilize informal, cumulative assessments such as documentation panels, portfolios, and narrative notes, Learning Stories can provide an additional, complementary narrative-based form of authentic assessment. For programs and sites that feature mandated standardized assessments such as the Quality Rating Improvement Systems (QRIS), Classroom Assessment Scoring Systems (CLASS), Desired Results Developmental Profile (DRDP), Teaching Strategies Gold (TS Gold), Cor Advantage, or Environmental Rating Scores (ERS), Learning Stories have the potential to assist in evaluating program quality, positive socio-emotional classroom atmosphere, physical classroom environment, and children's developmental milestones. (See the Appendix A at the back of the book for a more complete description of these standardized assessments.)

Moving Toward Authentic Assessment and Critical Pedagogy for All Children and Families

> Stories illuminate knowledge in such a way that it connects to the roots of who we are as individuals and as a community.
>
> — Maenette K.P. Benham (2007, 513)

Stories retell information, provide life lessons and morals, entertain, argue, and provide cultural preservation and emotional support. As Benham (2007), notes, "stories illuminate knowledge in such a way that it connects to the roots of who we are as individuals and as a community" (513). For native and indigenous peoples, stories are told and retold to ensure that the ontology (what is known of the world) does not diminish; the story is sacred. Indigenous narratives are honest and in tune with the history of the earth, the land, animals, and people. This sacredness around stories entails a certain level of vulnerability for storytellers and audiences, who both must show respect for the privilege of entering into someone else's life, even if for a short period of time. In using Learning Stories in classrooms and other settings this experience occurs as teachers enter into the intimate space of stories for children, other teachers, and families. In turn, families enter into the thinking space of teachers. When writing classroom stories where children are the protagonists of their own learning, teachers highlight their personal and community values, such as respect, collaboration, and trust, and, perhaps more importantly, they open the door for a meaningful dialogue, exchange, and communication with the intent to get to know children better.

The power of narrative in Learning Stories to define what is real in the context of classrooms and school communities can be either a means to illuminate and support an entire community or an instrument to diminish it. We have chosen to use the benefit of storytelling and narrative to tell stories that uplift the image of young children, as well as that of their families and teachers. Voices of young children, their families, and their educators are not often heard in

US society; the examples in this book represent these voices and also come from communities of color and people working with special education services.

The Learning Story journey starts by honoring the sacredness of the process of telling and listening. When you actively engage in telling and listening to the stories of your children, families, and communities, you can learn much about who you are and how you can form collaborative learning communities. For example, three years ago, on a study trip to New Zealand, I (author Isauro) learned firsthand about the sacredness of storytelling when an early childhood teacher sang a brief ceremonial song prior to sitting down to share a welcoming story with the children, his co-teachers, and study tour visitors. This ceremonial singing was part of the Maori tradition to welcome visitors into their school grounds, and it is called a *pōwhiri*, a Maori welcoming ceremony. First there's a *karanga*, an exchange of calls that takes place while the visitors are entering the *marae* (meeting grounds) of a tribe or family. This is followed by a *haka pōwhiri*, a ceremonial song and dance during which the visitors are symbolically drawn into the *marae*. The song could well be about drawing in a canoe but symbolically they're drawing in their guests. Through these ceremonies, a new community is formed.

Learning Stories That Embrace Who We Are

Children from culturally and ethnically diverse backgrounds are frequently expected to conform to and learn in cultural settings that vastly differ from those they have experienced in their households, families, home countries, and communities (Souto-Manning & Mitchell 2010). As is the case with many immigrant families from Mexico and Central America and elsewhere, some children and their families may have never been exposed to the mainstream norms of the dominant US culture, yet are expected to adapt to those norms and live up to those expectations in early childhood teaching and assessments. For example, regardless of how long families have been in the United States, 4-year-old children in state-funded preschools must be formally tested in nursery rhyme knowledge based on traditional American children's songs and rhymes such as "Twinkle, Twinkle, Little Star" and "Teddy Bear, Teddy Bear, Turn Around." In this part of the phonological assessment, the assessor recites lines from ten different nursery rhymes and pauses, prompting the child to supply the final rhyming words. Usually, children of immigrant families are expected to immediately and successfully engage in dominant and unfamiliar cultural practices to be considered prepared for school, ready or capable (Bennett et al. 2018; Ghiso 2016; Souto-Manning 2009).

Successfully bridging children's emergent bicultural and bilingual identities depends on culturally responsive teaching practices that strengthen teachers' relationships with children and their families through understanding and making visible their interests, language, cultures, beliefs, and customs (Gay 2002; Hammond 2014; Ladson-Billings 2014). One key pathway is for teachers to support authentic assessment and a transformative curriculum by making pedagogical space for children's and families' funds of knowledge (Ghiso 2016; Gonzalez, Moll, & Amanti 2005; Licona 2013; Llopart & Esteban-Guitart 2018; Esteban-Guitart, Lalueza, Zhang-Yu, & Llopart 2019.). These funds of knowledge are the strategies, abilities, practices, and ideas that children and families rely on in their familial networks and for social and cultural authenticity and preservation (Souto-Manning & Mitchell 2010). Learning Stories in many ways may be considered a manifestation of the funds of knowledge that children, their families, and teachers bring with them into their classrooms and school communities. As such, Learning Stories break the traditional unhealthy balance of power between teachers and parents. For example, in traditional observation tools teachers as experts offer their informed opinions on children's development, progress, and growth without room for parents' perspectives on their own child, whereas in Learning Stories teachers as partners offer their points of view and parents contribute by writing or sharing with teachers and their own children what they see as valuable in the learning experiences. Learning Stories offer families the symbolic and practical space to voice their opinions on their children as continuous learners. The families' words are preserved in their own handwritten notes as a critical component of the children's Learning Stories. In the funds of knowledge and Learning Stories contexts, families are thought of as intellectual resources and competent people, no matter what their social, linguistic, religious, economic or cultural background may be (Llopart & Esteban-Guitart 2018; Rodriguez 2013).

Foundational Principles for Learning Stories

What exactly is a Learning Story? A Learning Story is first and foremost a story (Carr & Lee 2012). It tells a tale written to the child that is meant to be shared with the family. To some extent, it is also a tale told to the school community and to educators themselves. Each story is based on teachers' daily observations of children at play. It is always written from a strength-based perspective and, although there is not a universal template or blueprint to create a Learning Story, there are three basic principles at the foundation of any Learning Story:

1. To include written observations and photographs of children in action or of artifacts they created
2. To include a written analysis of the observation from the teachers' point of view
3. To provide a tentative plan to extend children's learning, pending the families' perspective on their child's learning experience
4. Optional: To include specific links to evaluative outcomes

Keep these four basic principles in mind as you collect material for a possible Learning Story, and then again as you prepare for the actual writing and creation of a Learning Story for children and their families.

Basic Components in Writing a Learning Story

Given the foundational principles just discussed, what do Learning Stories look like and what are their basic components? While the format or structure of Learning Stories may vary in US contexts, as they do in New Zealand and elsewhere globally, we (the authors) have found one format to be effective, yet flexible (Drummond n.d.; Carter 2010).

KEY IDEA

Key Idea: The Basic Components of a Learning Story

1. Title: A title that captures the essence of the story
2. "What Happened?" or "What's the Story?": A detailed observation of the event that took place
3. "What Does It Mean?" or "What Learning Do I See Happening?": A paragraph to reflect and interpret the significance of what was observed
4. "Opportunities and Possibilities" or "How Can We Support You in Your Learning": A paragraph to describe what teachers may potentially do to extend the child's learning experiences
5. "What's the Family's Perspective": A question posed to the family to respond with their point of view to what the teacher wrote
6. Assessment measures: At the end, quite often but not always, teachers link the learning story to specific evaluative and assessment measures, such as some of the 43 measures listed in the DRDP-r 2015 rating scale.

Title

Any great story begins with a good title that captures the essence of the tale being told. Although it is not unusual to create the title as the first step in writing the story if teachers have a firm idea of what aspect of the child's learning they want to highlight in the Learning Story, Margie Carter (2010) suggests that the act of giving a title to the story be saved for the end, after the teacher has written, reflected on, and analyzed the significance of what has been observed. In any case, the title has to reflect the child as a competent learner or highlight an aspect of the Learning Story that reveals the teacher, as much as possible, reflecting on his or her own learning as a result of observing the child and interpreting the learning that took place. In this sense, the Learning Story may serve as a reflection tool for both adult and child where the roles of teacher and learner are not static, but interchangeable. Along with the title, it is equally important to include who wrote the Learning Story and when.

"What Happened?" or "What's the Story?"

In this paragraph, the teacher begins the story with his or her own interest in what the child has taken the initiative to do, describing what the child does and says. The teacher writes in the first person using "I," which brings a personal perspective that is essential to the tale, writing directly to the child. For example, " Miguel, yesterday I noticed that you . . . ." or "Gaby, today I heard you say . . . ." or "Nathan, this morning I saw you . . . ." The teacher describes what the child does and says from the perspective of someone who deeply cares and is listening closely to discover what is actually happening and the learning that is taking place. It is important to note that quite often, this description is not totally objective. The teacher is present with his or her own feelings. Usually, the teacher includes his or her first name so the child and the family will know who wrote the story. The author's name can be included right underneath the title or at the end of the story.

When creating a Learning Story, it is helpful to describe the environment where the events took place, including the time of the day, the context where the events took place, and who was interacting with the child at that particular time. Other information to consider includes the materials the child or children were using, how they were engaging with those materials, and whether there was a practical or intellectual challenge that the children encountered and how they went about to resolve it. Describing the process in as much detail as possible, with the aid of a few photographs or brief video and a few anecdotal notes, will be quite useful later to help put the story together.

"What Does It Mean" or "What Learning Do I See Happening?"

"What does it mean?" or "What learning do I see happening?" are questions to encourage teachers to reflect, interpret, and write about the significance of what was observed. The photographs, video or audio recordings, or transcripts of the child in action serve as evidence of the child's resourcefulness, skills, dispositions, and talents. Meaning making is best done in a dialogue with other teachers, because including multiple perspectives, or multiple pedagogical opinions of events, paints a more objective picture that also becomes richer and more nuanced. When asked about the subjective nature of Learning Stories, Margaret Carr and Wendy Lee (2012, 2019) usually state that objectivity is more likely to be reached when multiple voices or perspectives are included in the Learning Story.

"Opportunities and Possibilities" or "How Can We Support You in Your Learning?"

The "Opportunities and Possibilities" section, which addresses the question "How can we support you in your learning?", offers a space where teachers describe what they can tentatively do the next day or during the next few days to scaffold and extend the child's learning and envision what the near and far future may hold. This is the area where teachers may offer possible activities to plan with the child or children about what to do next to co-create a meaningful curriculum connected to an individual child's or group of children's genuine interests. This gives insight to the participants and stakeholders in the school about how teachers actively think about what they do as practitioners to plan meaningful individualized activities, respecting the child's or children's agency. These activities might include gathering books on certain topics, searching for information on the internet, planning a field trip, collecting specific materials, and so on.

"What's the Family's Perspective?"

Ideally, a question is posed to the child's family to respond in writing with their point of view and reaction to what the teacher(s) wrote, but this can also be accomplished in a one-on-one conversation with the parents, or even in an email or text message exchange, if the parents prefer. This component is in a way an open invitation for the family to offer their perspective on how they see their child as a competent learner. Quite often, the child's family responds to the teacher and sometimes, when the teachers ask parents to reply directly to the child, they write very personal and heartfelt messages to their children, as we will see in different examples throughout the book. It is not uncommon for parents to answer with a question to the teacher, which enriches the dialogue and strengthens the communication between home and school. Occasionally, the child's family even suggests ideas, activities, and materials to implement and use in the classroom to support their child's learning or to enhance the learning experiences for all the children and teachers in the class.

Learning Stories as Evaluation Tools

Assessment connections are usually made at the end, linking the Learning Story to specific evaluative measures required by the program, school district, or state, such as the Desired Results Developmental Profile-2015 (DRDP-r 2015) (see Appendix A at the back of the book). For example, it is here where teachers insert a list of some of the 43 measures that they noticed the children accomplished in the story being told. Some programs might choose to focus on the learning dispositions that are captured in the story rather than on the measures themselves, such as the child's resolve, determination, courage, persistence, curiosity, compassion, kindness, empathy, and so forth. The learning dispositions emphasized vary from school to school and from one community to the next. Learning dispositions reflect to some extent the values of the teachers, the school, and the larger community.

Although the basic story format might seem highly structured, it is most of all a guide for teachers looking for alternative ways to observe, assess and extend children's learning processes from a strength-based perspective. This proposed basic format helps teachers to organize fleeting ideas into a coherent narrative to make sense of an isolated or ongoing experience or event. It is important to have a flexible approach to this format, and vary this structure so that you can be as responsive as possible to the needs and talents of the teachers, children, and families involved in a Learning Story. For instance, there are occasions when children themselves want to respond to their families' response toward the end of the Learning Story, or teachers suggest that children and families write a response to the Learning Story together. We discuss these possibilities in other chapters in this book, for instance in Chapter 6 we focus on strategies to promote family responses and connections to Learning Stories. The basic Learning Story format should also remain open to the use of multiple languages, visuals, and a sense of aesthetics that reflect the talents and goals of educators creating the Learning Stories. In this sense, each Learning Story is a work of art, a gift from educators to children and their families, but it is also a testament and document that makes visible the care, dedication, and talents of educators themselves.

For instance, in the following Learning Story that I (author Isauro) wrote, "What's in a Name?" (Figure 2.1), I followed the basic Learning Story format discussed above, but I approached this Learning Story with my own particular goals for content, format, language, visuals, aesthetics, voice, audience, and sharing. These are all elements of narrative that I orchestrated as I created a Learning Story to document how and why 4-year-old Anna worked on learning to write her name. Originally written in Spanish, I later translated "What's in a Name?" into English. I wanted to make visible in a public way the story of how and why Anna integrated her knowledge about her name into her social, cultural, and linguistic identity and the learner she is becoming in our preschool classroom. The impetus for this story of her name originally came from her family in an oral story Anna was told at home and that she felt comfortable sharing at school.

¿Qué Es lo Que Hay en un Nombre?

Isauro M. Escamilla
Febrero 10, 2020

¿Cuál Es la Historia?

Anna, la semana pasada me preguntaste si sabía que ya puedes escribir tu nombre. Sí, ya lo sabía. Te había visto escribir tu nombre en varias ocasiones. Entonces, también me preguntaste: ¿Sabes lo que significa mi nombre? Honestamente, no lo sabía. Lo admití. Sonreíste y compartiste conmigo lo que sabes sobre tu nombre:

Anna: Mi nombre significa paz.
Maestra: ¿Cómo lo sabes?
Anna: Lo sé porque mi mamá me lo dijo, pero no recuerdo exactamente cuándo me lo dijo.
Maestro: Y según tú, ¿qué significa la palabra paz?
Anna: La paz significa ser amable, ser amiga de los demás, jugar con todos, amar a toda la familia y a todos tus compañeros. Además, significa ser amable con todos los demás. ¿Sabes que mi nombre se escribe con dos enes? A, n, n, a. Me gusta mi nombre porque significa paz. Mi mamá se llama Alejandra y cuando llegue a casa le preguntaré qué significa su nombre. Mi nombre suena así, a, a, a. Conozco a otra persona que se llama Ana, con una ene. Bueno, su nombre es Ana María y es la mamá de Allison. Mi mamá y Ana María son hermanas, hermanas de la Iglesia. Ana María no es mi tía. Solo tengo un tío que se llama Juan.

¿Qué Significa Esto?

Podría significar que estás muy consciente de quién eres y en quién te estás convirtiendo. El hecho de que tú, Anna, a los cuatro años, definas la palabra paz como un verbo de acción, es muy inspirador. Asocias la paz con ser amable, jugar y amar. Esas tres palabras deberían describir el mundo en el que crecen todos los niños. Como maestros, tenemos la responsabilidad de crear un ambiente escolar tranquilo donde tú y tus compañeros aprendan a ser amables y jugar, y querer y respetarse unos a otros. ¡Tenemos mucho que aprender de ti!

¿Cómo Podemos Extender Tu Aprendizaje?

Anna, como una forma de apoyarte para expresar tus ideas más allá de la palabra hablada, te invité a escribir tu nombre y los nombres de los miembros de tu familia. Escribiste *Alejandra*, el nombre de tu mamá; *Ana María*, el nombre de la hermana de tu mamá; *Francisco*, el nombre de tu papá y *Juan*, el nombre de tu tío. Ahora, gracias a ti, ¡sé los nombres de todos en tu familia! Se dice que tenemos familia cercana y parientes lejanos, pero en realidad todos son familia y es todo lo que tenemos, familia. Me alegro mucho que tu mamá haya encontrado una hermana en la mamá de Allison.

Anna, además de escribir los nombres de los miembros de tu familia, también hiciste un dibujo de todos ellos y anotaste sus nombres. ¡Gracias por compartir tu historia, dibujar y escribir! ¿Puedo compartir algo contigo? Yo también tengo un hermano y una hermana. Sus nombres son Antonio y Martha. Nati y Rodrigo son los nombres de mi mamá y mi papá y los quiero mucho.

Comentarios de la Señora Alejandra, la Madre de Anna

Encontré el nombre de mi hija en la Biblia. Me gustaba Anna como nombre para mi hija porque significa "Mujer de Paz." Anna también tiene un segundo nombre, que es Ruth y también proviene de la Biblia. Ruth significa "Buena Compañera." Estas son cualidades que vienen con un nombre dado que es de la Biblia. Dios lo bendiga. Gracias.

Figure 2.1 Original Learning Story in Spanish and English "Qué Es lo Que Hay en un Nombre?" "What's in a Name?" by Isauro M Escamilla

What's in a Name?

Isauro M. Escamilla
February 10, 2020

Anna, last week you asked me if I knew that you already know how to write your name. Yes, I did. I had seen you write your name quite a few times. Then, you also asked me: *Do you know what my name means?* Honestly, I didn't know. You smiled and shared with me what you know about your name:

Anna: My name means *peace*.
Teacher: How do you know?
Anna: I know because my mom told me, but I don't remember exactly when she told me.
Teacher: And according to you, what does the word *peace* mean?
Anna: *Peace* means being kind, being friends with others, playing with everyone, loving the entire family and all your peers. Also, it means to be nice to everyone else. Do you know that my name is written with two "n"s? A, n, n, a. I like my name because it means peace. My mom's name is Alejandra and when I get home, I'm going to ask her what her name means. My name sounds like this, a, a, a. I know another person named Ana, with one "n." Well, her name is Ana María and she is Allison's mother. My mom and Ana Maria are sisters, Church sisters. Ana María is not my aunt. I only have an uncle named Juan.

What Does This Mean?

It might mean that you are keenly aware of who you are and who you are becoming. The fact that you Anna, at four years old, defines the word *peace* as an action verb is very inspiring. You associate peace with being kind, with play, and love. Those three words should describe the world in which all children grow up. As teachers, we have a responsibility to create a peaceful school environment where you and your peers learn to be kind and playful, and love and respect each other. We have a lot to learn from you!

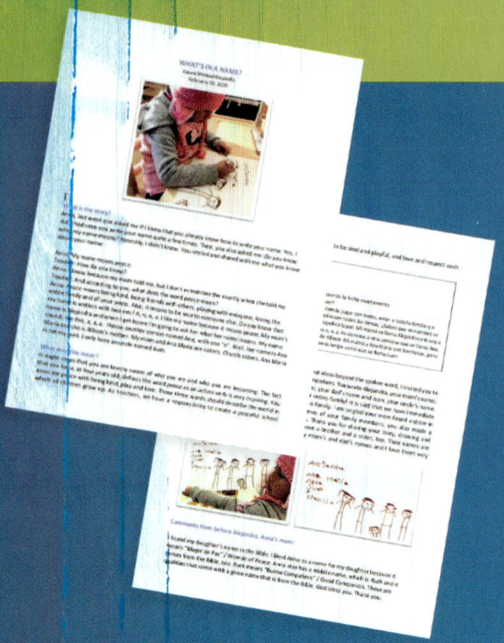

How Can We Extend Your Learning?

Anna, as a way to support you in expressing your ideas beyond the spoken word, I invited you to write your name and the names of your family members. You wrote Alejandra, your mom's name; Ana Maria, your mom's sister's name; Francisco, your dad's name, and Juan; your uncle's name. Now, thanks to you, I know the names of your entire family! It is said that we have immediate and extended family, but in reality, all we have is family. I am so glad your mom found a sister in Allison's mom. Anna, besides writing the names of your family members, you also made a drawing of all of them and listed their names. Thank you for sharing your story, drawing and writing! May I share something with you? I have a brother and a sister, too. Their names are Antonio and Martha. Nati and Rodrigo are my mom's and dad's names and I love them very much!

Comments from Señora Alejandra, Anna's Mom

I found my daughter's name in the Bible. I liked *Anna* as a name for my daughter because it means "Mujer de Paz" / Woman of Peace. Anna also has a middle name, which is *Ruth*, and it comes from the Bible, too. *Ruth* means "Buena Compañera" / Good Companion. These are qualities that come with a given name that is from the Bible. God bless you. Thank you.

Figure 2.1 Continued.

"What's in a Name?" shows evidence of the four basic principles of a Learning Story. First, I knew from creating Learning Stories over the last four years within the context of my school's collaborative inquiry group that rich and vibrant written observations and visuals are critical for a compelling and meaningful Learning Story. They draw us into the story and, like in a well-told picture book for young children, I try to have the text and the visuals each work on their own as well as together, to complement each other.

For instance, in what I wrote, I tried to give Anna as much voice and visibility as possible, describing her actions, and also highlighting her Spanish language use, her thoughts, her ideas, and the manner in which she explained the origin of her name and her deep connections with her family and community. In the visuals, I took a number of photographs as I always do, and I selected those that I felt showed evidence of Anna's actual writing and art, her close physical proximity to the whiteboard, and her relationship to the symbols of what she had just created. I also wanted these visuals to counter the prevailing depiction of young children of color who are learning English that they don't have the requisite determination or knowledge to acquire traditional, school-based literacy skills. The visuals that I selected, then, depict Anna as a strong and determined writer, artist, symbol maker, and symbol explainer.

Second, I analyzed and reflected upon how this Learning Story captures Anna's devotion to language as the center of her identity and social relationships both at school and at home. I did not quite realize the importance of this for Anna, and even the other children, until I gathered the material for this Learning Story and wrote it. I then saw more clearly how Anna uses this moment in her learning, linking her name and her identity, as a form of linking her funds of knowledge about her family and literacy with what Vygotsky (1978) calls the zone of proximal development, which is a series of developmental and pedagogical spaces in which children experiment, problem-solve, and learn on their own and with others. This is why I wrote, "It might mean that you are keenly aware of who you are and who you are becoming." I realized that Anna had a developmentally and culturally relevant series of moments of showing herself, me, and her family how her deep connection to her name also connected her with her larger social, cultural, and literary world.

Third, I considered a few important next steps for Anna's learning. Prior to the experience of this name writing and drawing, I was not as aware of Anna's deep interest in personal literacy making, and the creation of the Learning Story provoked me to consider possible next steps for Anna's continued learning and growth. I describe in the Learning Story how I made some changes in my thinking and instruction during this experience with Anna—"Anna, as a way to support you in expressing your ideas beyond the spoken word, I invited you to write your

More Story Insights

Besides the cultural richness, this story also contains elements of language and literacy development that are evident in Anna's ability to understand, respond, and communicate complex ideas such as explaining the way she is related to her immediate and extended family and community in general. Anna demonstrates interest in literacy by her willingness to attempt writing the letters of her name and the names of her parents Alejandra and Francisco, uncle Juan, and aunt Ana María. Anna seems familiar with print concepts and writes names in a list from left to right. Anna makes visible that she knows how to trace letters and that letters only gain meaning when they spell a word, in this case a word to which Anna has a strong emotional attachment, such as the names of her family members. When Anna reads the names on her list she demonstrates letter and word knowledge, and this sample of her drawing and writing can certainly be considered evidence of her emergent writing skills, which will only improve with more practice. This combination of drawing, writing, and storytelling provides a great literacy foundation that will become quite useful for Anna when she transitions to kindergarten next fall.

name and the names of your family members." Later, upon further reflection, I then saw how important it was for Anna to link the writing and drawing of her name with those of family members. I realized that at the time I did not reciprocate and fully join in with Anna in her learning, and that I could have shared with Anna the names of my siblings: "May I share something with you? I have a brother and a sister, too. Their names are Antonio and Martha. Nati and Rodrigo are my mom's and dad's names, and I love them very much!" While the Learning Story shows how I realized that I did not make a deep enough social and cultural connection with Anna's interests, I also now see that I could have added more new ideas for deepening Anna's learning. I could have, for instance, added an idea for Anna to help teach other children how to write their names; possibly, I could provide Anna with a list of the children's names and she could work with interested children on writing their names, and then drawing pictures of their family members and friends. I could also help the children dictate some of their ideas and stories, and write them down in Spanish, and then compile their responses in a book for sharing and discussion with the other children. The addition of other instructional next steps would also offer more food for thought for my colleagues to comment on when I presented this Learning Story at one of our collaborative inquiry group meetings.

Fourth, I thought about links to assessments. This Learning Story reveals Anna's growth in the socio-emotional and literacy areas, which are related to specific DRDP measures, as shown in Table 2.1.

In this story Anna shows a strong sense of self-identity in relation to her closest family members (mom, dad, and uncle) and members of her extended family (Ana María and her daughter, Allison). Anna seems to be quite aware that although Ana María and Allison are not blood related, they still share a strong emotional bond. In fact, Anna shares that Ana María and her mom are sisters brought together by the spiritual bond that their church community provides. From conversations with Anna's mom the teachers have learned that she values her close relationship with Ana María, Allison's mom, and that her blood sister is back in Guatemala. Creating a support network through a church community is an asset that many immigrant families depend on for encouragement, care, companionship, and community building. This is another example of how families use their funds of knowledge to share resources and support each other in their communities.

Taken together, the four basic principles evident in the Learning Story represent one small, important connection linking authentic assessment and critical pedagogy. For example, I highlighted Anna's cultural, linguistic, and personal talents and interests in a public forum as I have done in this Learning

Social and Emotional Development (SED)	Language and Literacy Development (LLD)
1. Identity of Self in Relation to Others	1. Understanding of Language (Receptive)
2. Social and Emotional Understanding	2. Responsiveness to Language
3. Relationships and Social Interactions with Familiar Adults	3. Communication and Use of Language (Expressive)
4. Relationships and Social Interactions with Peers	4. Reciprocal Communication and Conversation
5. Symbolic and Sociodramatic Play	5. Interest in Literacy
	6. Comprehension of Age-Appropriate Text
	7. Concepts About Print
	8. Phonological Awareness
	9. Letter and Word Knowledge
	10. Emergent Writing

Table 2.1. Social and Emotional and Language and Literacy DRDP Measures

Story. The story is a public document and artifact that carries assessment "weight" and value, and it is a record of Anna's learning that can reach multiple audiences (children, families, teachers, administrators) and be made visible in multiple spaces (school, home, community).

Chapter Summary

This chapter described Learning Stories as an approach that educators can use to link authentic assessment and critical pedagogy. Learning Stories can be utilized in independent early childhood programs to complement existing narrative-based anecdotal records, portfolios, and documentation panels and binders. They can also be utilized in public early childhood contexts that feature multiple, mandated assessment measures such as the DRDP as a way to provide a powerful narrative form of documenting and reflecting on children's experiences, insights, developmental leaps, cultural affirmations, questions, and theories. This chapter also described the four foundational principles underlying Learning Stories, as well as the six basic components for structuring and organizing a Learning Story. The discussion of one Learning Story, "What's in a Name?", provided an example of how the basic principles and the six components are integrated into one document and product. It was also noted that creativity, flexibility, and personal flair and voice are to be emphasized in the creation of a Learning Story. When Learning Stories are told with a strong and authentic voice, and draw upon rich and vibrant observations and visuals, they most powerfully become an integrated mix of authentic assessment and critical pedagogy. In the next chapter, we discuss more specifically how educators can identify and collect potential material for the creation of Learning Stories.

Key Points

- Learning Stories are told by educators from a strength-based perspective, viewing the whole child as a person rather than fragmenting the child into separate parts based on predetermined assessment measures.
- Learning Stories offer families the symbolic and practical space to voice their opinions on their children as continuous learners.
- There are three basic principles at the foundation of any Learning Story that are critical to the success of the story as a form of assessment including (1) written observations and photographs of children in action or of artifacts they created, (2) written analysis of the observation from the teachers' point of view, (3) a tentative plan to extend children's learning, pending the families' perspective on their child's learning experience, and (4) specific links to evaluative outcomes.

References

Benham, M. 2007. "Mo'ōlelo: On Culturally Relevant Story Making from an Indigenous Perspective." In *Handbook of Narrative Inquiry: Mapping a Methodology*, ed. D.J. Clandinin, 512–534. Thousand Oaks, CA: Sage.

Bennett, S.V., A.A. Gunn, G. Gayle-Evans, E.S. Barrera, & C.B. Leung. 2018. "Culturally Responsive Literacy Practices in an Early Childhood Community." *Early Childhood Education Journal* 46 (2): 241–248.

Carr, M. 2001. *Assessment in Early Childhood Settings: Learning Stories*. Thousand Oaks, CA: Sage.

Carr, M., & W. Lee. 2012. *Learning Stories: Constructing Learner Identities in Early Education*. Thousand Oaks, CA: Sage.

Carr, M., & W. Lee. 2019. *Learning Stories in Practice*. Thousand Oaks, CA: Sage.

Carter, M. 2010. "Using Learning Stories to Strengthen Teachers' Relationships with Children." *Exchange* 32 (6): 40–44.

Carter, M. 2017. "Growing Ourselves as Leaders: A Conversation with Annie White." *Exchange*, November/December, 46–51.

Drummond, T. n.d. "Writing Learning Stories." Accessed December 27, 2020. https://tomdrummond.com/looking-closely-at-children/writing-learning-stories/

Esteban-Guitart, M., Lalueza, J. L., Zhang-Yu, C., & Llopart, M. (2019). "Sustaining students' cultures and identities. A qualitative study based on the funds of knowledge and identity approaches." *Sustainability*, 11 (12): 3400.

Gay, G. 2002. "Preparing for Culturally Responsive Teaching." *Journal of Teacher Education* 53 (2): 106–116.

Ghiso, M.P. 2016. "The Laundromat as the Transnational Local: Young Children's Literacies of Interdependence." *Teachers College Record* 118 (1): 1–46.

Gonzalez, N., L. Moll, & C. Amanti. 2005. *Theorizing Practices in Households, Communities, and Classrooms*. Mahwah, NJ: Erlbaum.

Hammond, Z. 2014. *Culturally Responsive Teaching and the Brain: Promoting Authentic Engagement and Rigor Among Culturally and Linguistically Diverse Students*. Thousand Oaks, CA: Corwin Press.

Ladson-Billings, G. 2014. "Culturally Relevant Pedagogy 2.0: a.k.a. The Remix." *Harvard Educational Review* 84 (1): 74–84.

Licona, M.M. 2013. "Mexican and Mexican-American Children's Funds of Knowledge as Interventions into Deficit Thinking: Opportunities for Praxis in Science Education." *Cultural Studies of Science Education* 8 (4): 859–872.

Llopart, M., & M. Esteban-Guitart. 2018. "Funds of Knowledge in 21st Century Societies: Inclusive Educational Practices for Under-Represented Students, A Literature Review." *Journal of Curriculum Studies* 50 (2): 145–161.

Meier, D. R., & A.J. Stremmel. 2010. "Reflection Through Narrative: The Power of Narrative Inquiry in Early Childhood Teacher Education." *Journal of Early Childhood Teacher Education* 31 (3): 249–257.

Rodriguez, G.M. 2013. "Power and Agency in Education: Exploring the Pedagogical Dimensions of Knowledge." *Review of Research in Education*, 37, 87–120.

Souto-Manning, M. (2009). "Negotiating Culturally Responsive Pedagogy Through Multicultural Children's Literature: Towards Critical Democratic Literacy Practices in a First Grade Classroom." *Journal of Early Childhood Literacy*, 9 (1), 50-74.

Souto-Manning, M., & C.H. Mitchell. 2010. "The Role of Action Research in Fostering Culturally-Responsive Practices in a Preschool Classroom." *Early Childhood Education Journal* 37 (4): 269.

Vygotsky, L.S. 1978. *Mind in Society: The Development of Higher Psychological Processes*. Cambridge, MA: Harvard University Press.

White, A. 2017. "Creating New Pathways for Dialogue: Collaboration of Diverse Voices." *NHSA Dialogue* 19 (1): 60–88. https://journals.uncc.edu/dialog/article/view/495/640

3

Identifying and Creating Learning Stories

We invite you to look at the stories, narratives, books, and quotes from young children's talk as a lens for exploring your own practice, drawing implications and exploring possibilities for your own class.

— Dana Franz Bentley and
Mariana Souto-Manning (2019, 44)

Opening Reflections

- How do Learning Stories help teachers to make visible children's learning over time, building on their interests, strengths, capabilities, and competencies?
- How can Learning Stories help teachers identify learning and teaching moments in their interactions with young children to shape the curriculum?
- Why is the analysis of Learning Stories so important to teachers as learners?

In adopting an inquiry stance, teachers wonder about their practice, including their students' learning and their own curriculum and interactions that promote this learning. By telling stories about these practices, teachers can identify Learning Stories (e.g., about curriculum, social interactions, or children's play), that communicate with children and families moments in a child's daily experience that highlight or illustrate important aspects of the child's learning and development. In this chapter we provide examples that show how teachers have identified these moments in their practice and then used the Learning Stories approach to support their inquiry into their own practices. The examples are taken from a public dual language preschool in San Francisco, California, where the teachers have been documenting children's learning by writing Learning Stories since 2017. The same teachers have been holding their monthly inquiry group meetings since 2010.

A Dual Language Preschool's Inquiry Group

School Background

Our preschool (authors Isauro Escamilla and Daniel Meier) is part of the San Francisco Unified School District (SFUSD) Early Education Department. A central goal of our program is to support the children's home languages and include family traditions, beliefs, and values in our curriculum through immersing children in Spanish or Cantonese, and English languages. Besides English, Spanish and Cantonese are the languages most commonly spoken in the school's neighborhood. Our dual language programs are quite inclusive and accept all students, even if the children or their families do not speak Spanish or Cantonese. After preschool, families might enroll their children in elementary schools with SFUSD's Spanish-English or Cantonese-English pathways, such as Dual Language Immersion, Biliteracy, Foreign Language in Elementary School, or Newcomer and Middle and High School World Languages. Families may also opt to enroll their children in monolingual English classrooms in public or private schools.

As early childhood educators in a state and federally funded preschool, serving children between 2.9 and 5.6 years old, we are required to conduct ongoing classroom observations to document and assess children's learning. The need for teachers to get together and discuss issues that truly matter to us led to the formation of our monthly staff meetings to reflect on our observation and documentation strategies. These monthly gatherings to talk about our pedagogical practices related to specific children, teachers, and classrooms later became known as our inquiry group meetings. The next section describes the beginnings of our inquiry group journey.

Teacher Inquiry and Learning Stories

About ten years ago at the early childhood program where I (Isauro) work, teachers requested to be free of classroom duties one afternoon a month, only four hours, to discuss topics that had to do with our situated pedagogies, that is, issues tightly related to processes and practices of teaching and learning involved in working with young children. The school district had allocated funds for each teacher to have one hour of prep time per week; we requested to get instead a substitute teacher for each one of us to work four hours so we could meet with colleagues on site.

Two prior site administrators did not endorse the idea, perhaps because it was coming from teachers and not from the top administration. One of these site administrators counterproposed that she produce the agenda and facilitate the meeting, like a traditional staff meeting. We, the teachers, expressed that the meeting we were envisioning was not to talk about or do paperwork, but rather to reflect on and discuss curriculum ideas, documentation of children's learning, and the challenges and successes of our work. We wanted a way to seek and support each other in our professional growth, since we felt that the formal outside trainings we were receiving through the district were too generic, repetitive, and without our teachers' input. The third site administrator, Mr. Hollands, who came on board two years later, agreed to our proposal and participated in our initial monthly inquiry group meetings, as we named these gatherings. Mr. Hollands continued to support the group, finding "our group provides a unique scholarly forum for teacher-initiated inquiry, in depth observations, and interpretation and discourse, which only improve the teaching/learning experience of both teachers and students" (Perry, Henderson, & Meier 2012, 178).

Over time, the school's inquiry group has expanded, and besides the six permanent early childhood educators, now it also includes two instructional coaches with a focus on second language learning, two teachers from the special education classroom (whose perspective has influenced teachers' views on documenting the learning of children with limited speech or mobility abilities, for example), and occasional participation of the current principal. The group has always had the voluntary support of a university professor as the group's outside pedagogical mentor, who helps to co-facilitate the inquiry group's meetings and co-plan the monthly agendas based on teacher's interests.

During our inquiry group meetings, we pay close attention to individual teachers' participations because we believe that a colleague's documentation provides an opportunity to look into specific questions of teaching and learning or new revelations about an individual child's learning journey. The teachers have learned that documentation or evidence of children's learning may be manifested in multiple ways such as:

- Anecdotal notes
- Entries in teacher journals
- Photographs (mostly taken with smartphones) of children in action
- Teachers' plans to extend children's learning, including field trips, materials, and activities
- Brief videos that capture children engaged with people, materials, places, and objects
- Examples of children's constructions, artwork, scribbles, and writing
- Transcripts of children's conversations, dialogues, dictations, and reflections
- Booklets that tell classroom stories through narrative and photography

All these modes of documentation showcase the work and voice of early childhood educators and children to foster an image of teachers as inquirers and learners who also engage with each other within a community of mutual respect to improve teaching and learning practices. Taking an inquiry stance has led some teachers to explore the following questions in the monthly on-site inquiry group meetings: How can early childhood educators support and make visible children's emergent social, cultural, and linguistic identities?

And within this process, how can teachers embed story, narrative and photography to document children's growth and strengthen parents' participation in their children's school experiences?

This chapter further examines the use of Learning Stories (Carr 2001; Carr & Lee 2012, 2019) as a narrative-based formative assessment to highlight children's strengths, talents, abilities, hopes, and curiosity. Learning Stories aid teachers and children in co-developing a meaningful curriculum that draws from spontaneous events and planned activities and is based on the interests, expertise, knowledge, and aspiration of children, teachers, and families. The Learning Story journey starts by honoring the process of observing, listening, reflecting, writing, and sharing. All of this—what was observed, analyzed, and written, is captured in a story, a Learning Story that is first shared with coteachers in the classroom and later with other teachers in on-site inquiry group meetings where colleagues offer constructive feedback and ask clarifying questions about the writing process, the story composition, the family's response, insights about the child or children's growth, and ideas on how to extend children's ongoing exploration and learning. When teachers engage in sharing the Learning Stories they create, knowing how they are told, to whom, and why, they not only uncover who they are as individual teachers but also who they are as a teaching and learning community, developing a deeper appreciation of children's interactions in their play and a richer understanding of themselves and their practices as educators constructing meaning with young children.

Identifying and Writing a Learning Story

Learning Stories are ongoing records of children's lives in the school community and to some extent, these stories also reveal the values, beliefs, and professional stance of educators based on daily observations of children at play in classrooms and school communities. As mentioned in previous chapters, Learning Stories are visual and written narratives created by teachers about children's growth from a strength-based perspective. Although Learning Stories can be written for a group of children, as you will see in Chapter 4, the emphasis in this chapter and in the entire book is on single stories written about individual children to highlight their personal preferences, interests, talents, skills, and even hopes and dreams. In Chapter 2, we described the five foundational components of a Learning Story. The first three components, listed here, are the most important to start writing a story:

- An observation with accompanying photographs
- An analysis of the observation
- A plan to extend children's learning

These components don't have to be extensive. A short paragraph will suffice for the observation and analysis. A plan to extend the child's learning could be something as simple and as brief as a couple of tentative ideas. With time and practice, the other two components could be added:

- The families' perspective on their child's learning experience
- Links to specific evaluative measures

The suggested format for creating and writing a Learning Story can be accomplished individually, but we have found that sometimes it is a less challenging and a much more enjoyable task when the process becomes a collaborative effort shared among teachers working in the same classroom. Believing that everyone has a story to tell, teachers support one another by sharing photographs, video clips, and samples of children's quotes, questions, discoveries, or accomplishments witnessed during the school day. This initial exchange of ideas and images where teachers try to explain to each other what they saw, heard, photographed, or captured in videos is what leads to inquiry and specific questions such as: how can you support and make visible children's emergent social, cultural, and linguistic identities? And within this process, how can you embed story, narrative, and photography to document children's growth and strengthen parents' participation in their children's school experiences?

Sometimes during the course of our (authors Isauro and Daniel's) inquiry group meeting, one of us uses a tablet or laptop to capture what another teacher casually describes about what happened. During this initial sharing we ask questions to recall specific details such as:

- Where exactly did the event happen?
- Who was involved?
- What was the child's demeanor?
- Was there a problem to solve?
- If so, how was it solved?
- What surprised you the most?
- How does the described event enhance your view on the child as an active learner?
- Was there anything new that you learned about the child or yourself?

At other times, working in pairs, one of the teachers in the classroom takes notes while the other elaborates and recalls particular information and details, trying to recreate the events that took place, going back to the photographs, specific frames of video clips, or anecdotal notes we jotted down in our teacher journals. We recognize photographs and video clips as integral parts of the story, in fact, even indispensable in creating a Learning Story. These brief video clips, sometimes as short as 15 to 30 seconds long, usually show children in action, engaged with other children, building, constructing, exploring, doing what they naturally do on any given day at school. The photographs we take with our cell phones or tablets tell a story on their own, depicting children engaged in what they choose to do in the classroom, outside in the school yard or on field trips to nearby places. Sometimes, we zoom in on a specific child and take multiple photographs, trying to capture certain moments in a series of sequenced images that show, for example, how a painting was created, how a problem was solved, how much fun the child seemed to have on a field trip, or how a child achieved a new goal or overcame an obstacle.

The descriptive narratives in a Learning Story provide us with an alternative method to organize our individual and teaching team's observations. And in the process of sharing those observations, photographs, video clips, and samples of children's works (drawings, ideas, artifacts, etc.), we delight in what children discover, inquire about, and naturally do in their everyday play. It is important to elaborate on the meaning of *observation*, which for the most part, might imply a pre-planned effort to see children do something. It is perfectly fine to plan for a scheduled observation, but the type of observation that predominantly guides Learning Stories is unprompted events that take place at any given time at school. Quite often wonderful things happen throughout the day, since children are constantly discovering something new or making new connections in their interactions with other children, materials, or the environment. All this is to say that teachers must be equally ready to create a record of that which suddenly catches their attention. Both of the two Learning Stories included later in this chapter started with unprompted and fleeting events: Frankie bringing his favorite stuffed toy to school and a comment he made about his desire to have a piñata; Luna trying to make Genesis laugh by singing in the school yard surrounded by other children.

By creating records or documentation of seemingly random moments throughout the day, teachers preserve specific moments of children's lived experiences at school through photographs, videos and anecdotal notes of what children say or do; or the way they act, react, or behave in their everyday play. The photographs, videos, and teachers' journal entries document fleeting classroom moments that might be otherwise forgotten. These disjointed pieces of documentation gain relevance when teachers start putting together a Learning Story.

Stories Humanize the Lived Experiences of Children, Teachers, and Families

Educational activities with preschool children should be based on daily observations of children at play both in the classroom and outdoors, including teachers' reflections and, as much as possible, parents' perspectives on their children's learning. Depending on when families enroll their children, most 3- and 4-year-old children spend an average of two years in preschool. In the case of toddlers, they may join their class when they are 18 months old and stay there until they turn 36 months old. In that time, teachers may get to know the families quite well. It is not uncommon for teachers to ask parents what languages they know, where and how they learned them, and what their perceptions are about monolingualism and bilingualism, among other things, such as their family traditions and celebrations. Sometimes, it might take time for families to feel comfortable sharing their perspective, opinions, dreams, and hopes with teachers. Teachers ask those questions because it is important to acknowledge the expertise, knowledge, and wisdom that families bring with them. This knowledge base encompasses cultural and linguistic assets or funds of knowledge present in children's households (Moll, Soto-Santiago, & Schwartz 2013). At the same time, Learning Stories offer a space where teachers may share with families a little bit of who they are as human beings and professionals, the philosophies that guide their teaching and how they perceive their children as active, social, creative learners.

In this context, early childhood teachers play a crucial role in supporting young children in maintaining their family values, home languages, and cultural heritage as they start their educational journey. Perhaps the success of bridging the emergent cultural and linguistic identities of these young children depends on teachers and school systems that embrace culturally responsive teaching practices (Hammond 2014; Ladson-Billings 2014). These practices include and honor the funds of knowledge and cultural capital—values, beliefs, hopes, and dreams—of the children and families you serve and work with. The use of Learning Stories in early childhood education settings places classroom stories within the broader social context of school communities that work together towards more equitable and inclusive pedagogies. A foundational tenet of culturally responsive teaching is a constant quest for equity of voice, including the voices of children, parents, and teachers, moving away from scripted curricula and leaning towards place-based curricula, where children's and parents' ideas, experiences, and knowledge are embedded and given the credit they deserve.

KEY IDEA

Steps to Creating a Learning Story

1. Use of photographs
2. Use of video
3. Documenting children's spontaneous social interaction and friendship
4. Teacher inquirer engages with the children and observes and documents
5. Teacher revisits events, reflects on tentative meanings
6. Teacher selects images that visually tell the story
7. Teacher starts writing and creating the Learning Story
8. Teacher shares the Learning Story with inquiry group to get feedback
9. Teacher incorporates feedback and edits story
10. Teacher shares Learning Story with children's family

The suggested structure to create and write a Learning Story helps teachers in organizing fleeting ideas into a coherent narrative to make sense of specific children's experiences or classroom observations. More importantly, the writing of Learning Stories encourages preschool teachers to showcase young children as competent explorers and linguistic learners in familiar settings at any given moment during the school day. When a teacher writes a story to the child the purpose is not to test a hypothesis or to evaluate, although the story could certainly be utilized to identify developmental milestones with links to specific assessment measures (see Appendix A at the back of the book), as is exemplified in Luna and Genesis' story written by teacher Sahara Gonzalez.

At the root of writing a Learning Story is an authentic interest in understanding children's lived experiences and the meaning teachers, families, and children themselves make of those experiences. Through Learning Stories teachers engage in pedagogical and intellectual work, humanizing the early childhood profession, moving towards more inclusive modes of observing, analyzing, and understanding the complexities of children's actions and behaviors. At the same time, children engage in making sense of the world around them and in doing so, start shaping or continue to form their own social, cultural, and linguistic identities.

Learning Stories that Capture Children's Lived Experiences

The following two Learning Stories, "Luna and Genesis: Making Genesis Smile," and "Francisco, Nemo, and His Piñata," were written by teachers Sahara Gonzalez and Isauro M. Escamilla, respectively. In these stories you will notice that teachers listen with intention and observe how children play, interact, and learn. Listening and observing with an inquiry lens helps teachers to focus on what children say and do by writing brief notes, taking a few photographs, or video recording their actions.

Luna's Learning Story: Friendship Between Luna and Genesis

"Luna and Genesis: Making Genesis Smile" is a two-page Learning Story that documents the interactions between Luna and Genesis and showcases the strong emotional connection between them. Luna and Genesis are two 4-year-old girls, apparently separated by classrooms, physical abilities, and speech and language skills, but, as teacher Sahara noticed, united by a friendship based on mutual understanding and affection for each other. Genesis uses a wheelchair with straps that support her torso, and she has impaired speech and limited vision. Whenever Luna came near her, Genesis became alert and responsive: her eyes seemed to become brighter, she smiled more, and she extended her arms as if trying to reach and touch Luna. A few adults took notice of Genesis's reaction to Luna's presence. They also noticed the way in which Luna's reserved demeanor gave room to a more expressive, outspoken side of Genesis's personality. Teacher Sahara used her cell phone to photograph and video record the interaction between the two little girls. She first took three or four photos and captured in a short video Luna's attempt to engage Genesis in counting, singing, and clapping while jumping up and down to the rhythm of her own beat (Figure 3.1).

More Story Insights

The original Luna and Genesis's Learning Story does not include the perspective of Genesis's parents, but many days later they did contribute to the story by writing to teachers a note in Spanish, which has been translated into English. Their thoughtful reflection served as an incentive for teacher Sahara to continue writing Learning Stories.

Luna and Genesis: Making Genesis Smile

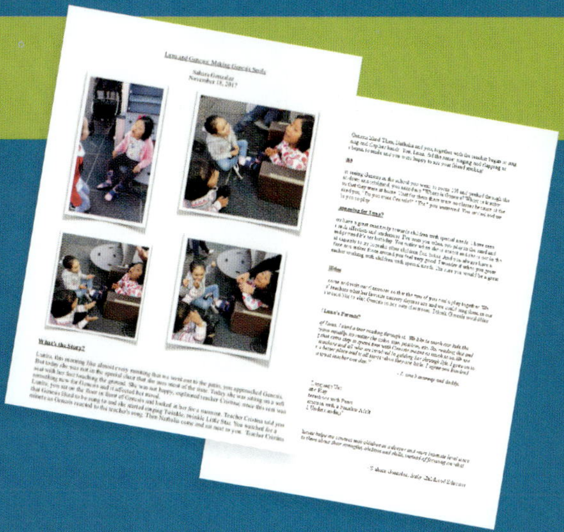

Sahara Gonzalez
November 18, 2017

Lunita, this morning like almost every morning that we went out to the patio, you approached Genesis. But today she was not in the special chair that she uses most of the time. Today she was sitting on a soft seat with her feet touching the ground. She was not happy, explained teacher Cristina; since this seat was something new for Genesis and it affected her mood.

Lunita, you sat on a the floor in front of Genesis and looked at her for a moment. Teacher Cristina told you that Genesis liked to be sung to and she started singing Twinkle, Twinkle Little Star. You watched for a minute as Genesis reacted to the teacher's song. Then Nathalia came and sat next to you. Teacher Cristina told both of you what song Genesis liked. Then, Nathalia and you, together with the teacher began to sing. Then, Genesis also tried to sing and clap her hands. You, Luna, did the same; singing and clapping as Genesis was doing. Genesis began to smile, and you were happy to see your friend smiling!

"Where Is Genesis?" — Luna

Luna, after a few days of not seeing Genesis in the school you went to room 101 and peeked through the window, the lights were shut down and intrigued, you asked me, "Where is Genesis? Where is teacher Cristina?" I explained to you that they were at home. That for them there were no classes because of the Thanksgiving holidays. I asked you, "Do you miss Genesis?" "Yes, " you answered. You smiled and we walked to the playground for your to play.

What Learning Do I See Happening for Luna?

Luna, I have noticed that you have a great sensitivity towards children with special needs. I have seen how you treat Genesis with such affection and tenderness. I've seen you when you play in the sand and prepare cakes for Genesis and pretend it's her birthday. You notice when she is absent and she is not in the schoolyard. You have a great capacity to try to make other children feel better. And you always have a smile that illuminates your face and makes those around you feel very good. I wonder if when you grow up you would like to be a teacher working with children with special needs. I'm sure you would be a great teacher!

Opportunities and Possibilities

We could invite Genesis to come and visit our classroom so that the two of you could play together. We could find out from Genesis' teachers what her favorite nursery rhymes are and we could sing them in our classroom. Or perhaps you would like to visit Genesis in her own classroom. I think Genesis would like that very much!

What's the Perspective of Luna's Parents?

"We are extremely proud of Luna. I shed a tear reading through it. We like to teach our kids the importance of treating everyone equally, no matter the color, size, position, etc. So, reading this and actually seeing Luna taking that extra step to spend time with Genesis means so much to us. We are thankful for our family, her teachers and all who are involved in guiding her through life. It goes to show that this world can be a better place and it all starts when they are little. I agree one hundred percent that Luna could be a great teacher one day."
— Luna's mommy and daddy.

DRDP Measures

1. Communication and Language Use
2. Symbolic and Dramatic Play
3. Relationships and Interactions with Peers
4. Relationship and Interactions with a Familiar Adult
5. Social and Emotional Understanding

Final Reflection

"Writing Learning Stories helps me connect with children at a deeper and more intimate level since I'm writing directly to them about their strengths, abilities and skills, instead of focusing on what they cannot do."
— Sahara Gonzalez, Early Childhood Educator

Figure 3.1 Original Learning Story "Luna and Genesis: Making Genesis Smile," by Sahara Gonzalez

More Story Insights

Wow! Estoy sorprendida y feliz por el lindo gesto de Luna hacia Génesis. Luna es una niña maravillosa y ejemplar. Tienes un gran corazón. Admiro muchísimo tu forma de ser y agradezco el cariño e interés que tienes por Génesis. Eres ejemplo para muchas personas. Estoy segura que tú puedes ser una gran maestra en el futuro.

Génesis tú también eres una niña maravillosa. Te has ganado el corazón de Luna y de muchas personas. Tu discapacidad no es impedimento para demostrar el cariño y amor hacia ellos. Eres una niña con un corazón muy grande, eres muy inteligente. Estoy segura que con el apoyo de personas como Luna llegarás muy lejos.

Adelso y Floridalma, Padres de Genesis

Wow! I am surprised and happy for such a nice gesture from Luna towards Genesis. Luna is a wonderful and exemplary girl. You have a big heart. I greatly admire the way you are and I appreciate the love and interest you have for Genesis. You are an example for many people. I'm sure you can be a great teacher in the future.

Genesis, you are also a wonderful girl. You have won Luna's heart and the heart of many other people. Your disability is not an impediment to show affection and love. You are a little girl with a very big heart, you are very intelligent. I'm sure that with the support of people like Luna you'll get very far.

Adelso and Floridalma, Parents of Genesis

The parents' responses to the Learning Stories teachers in our (authors Isauro Escamilla and Daniel Meier's) school write have changed over time. In the beginning, the parents would write a reply to the teachers, thanking us for sharing specific learning moments of their children at school, and although this was really appreciated, we felt it would be more powerful if they wrote a message directly to their children, just like teachers did. To achieve this goal, we began adding a brief prompt that read something like this: "After reading this Learning Story, what would you say to your child? Please write a few lines directly to Luna." This is another way to strengthen the relationship between children and parents and between parents and teachers.

Luna and Genesis's Learning Story was also shared at an individualized education program (IEP) meeting with Genesis's support team, which included her parents and special education teacher, a speech pathologist, a physical therapist, an occupational therapist, a nurse, a psychologist, and the school's principal. Often, IEP meetings tend to focus on what children cannot yet do on their own and present children as individual learners whose identity is determined within the parameters of percentiles, scales, and performance on standardized testing.

A Learning Story, on the other hand, offers a view of children as a celebration of their accomplishments and in relation to peers, places, and things.

When the learning story of the emergent friendship between Luna and Genesis was read aloud and a board with photographs of the story was displayed at the start of the IEP meeting, the team of professionals learned something new about Genesis. Genesis was actually engaged with Luna and tried as much as possible to make eye contact with Luna. Genesis also made the efforts to move within the confinements of her new chair to the rhythm of Luna's singsong voice while Luna counted from one to ten, jingled

KEY IDEA

Foundational Elements in this Learning Story

1. Use of photographs
2. Use of video
3. Documenting social interaction and friendship
4. Teacher inquirer engages with the children *and* observes *and* documents

the bell shakers, and jumped up and down in front of Genesis. A video clip of the joyful interaction between Genesis and Luna showed Genesis as responsive, excited, genuinely interested, and cheerful. The straightforward language used in the story, the tender tone of the teacher's voice in the narrative, the brief videos of Genesis interacting with Luna, and the photographs as illustrations of the story touched many of the adults' hearts and hopefully, helped to humanize the IEP meeting, placing relationships at the core of young children's education.

Francisco's Learning Story: Frankie and His Nemo Piñata

The following four-page Learning Story, written by Isauro, tells the story of four-year-old Francisco (Frankie), whose favorite movie character is Nemo from the Disney film *Finding Nemo*. Frankie's Learning Story was originally written in Spanish, which is the language that his mom, dad, and 6-year-old sister mostly speak at home. In this particular Learning Story, I (Isauro) also share information about my own childhood memories. This Learning Story serves as a means to communicate with Frankie's family their child's interests and to show how he participated in classroom activities by leading the way to design and make a piñata for everyone in his class. Frankie demonstrated detailed knowledge of Nemo's characteristics and undertook the role of expert. He observed and shared that Nemo is orange with a large white stripe and one black line all around. Frankie exhibited leadership when he remembered to bring Nemo to school the next day for his classmates and teachers to see what it looked like. He expressed an inquiry by asking if we could buy a Nemo piñata at the store, and he showed his excitement with the idea of making a piñata from scratch at school, for which the children used their own hands, recycled newspaper, a balloon, and a homemade paste. My recollections of growing up in Mexico and how homemade piñatas were used on special occasions in my childhood served as a springboard to plan specific activities based on Frankie's interest and gradually involved more children over several days.

Frankie's Learning Story documents his love for a fictional character, Nemo, and his desire to have fun breaking a piñata. I worked with his other teachers as a team, each taking different roles to support the process of making a piñata in which many children took part. This is a good example of how an individual child's interest might invite other children to participate at different times in spontaneous and semi-structured activities. Frankie's idea prompted a whole-class project that required us to check out informational books from the library, engage in shared reading, access YouTube videos, and design and decorate the piñata according to Frankie's knowledge of Nemo's shape, colors, and size (Figure 3.2).

More Story Insights

The culminating event for this class project coincided with celebrating the upcoming winter break and hopefully, through these spontaneous and planned activities, the children were left with an appreciation for a tradition that is celebrated in many Latin American countries, a tradition that has been brought north and that is worth preserving for generations to come.

The children's genuine interest in the process of making a piñata from scratch motivated teachers to collaborate and gather information from fiction and non-fiction books and from the internet on how to make the children's vision a reality.

Inquiry Groups: Pedagogical Spaces for Change

Inquiry groups could be defined as pedagogical spaces and professional learning communities that seek, among other things, to counteract the constant drive toward standardization of learning and test-driven assessments and to link classroom practices with reflective teaching, where teachers examine how their values on human dignity, participation, openness to uncertainty, and democracy (Curtis & Carter 2017) influence the way they teach and learn with and from each other and young children. Inquiry groups afford early childhood educators the possibilities and opportunities to discuss school issues related to curriculum, culture, language,

Francisco, Nemo, and His Piñata!

Isauro M. Escamilla
November 12, 2019

What Is the Story?

Francisco, In the first days you started coming to our school we noticed that you are a talkative child. One morning you said that one of your favorite movies and characters is Nemo. You told me you liked Nemo because he's a good friend and is pretty. You asked me if I knew him. I replied that indeed I knew who Nemo was, an orange fish with black stripes. You looked at me with a puzzled look and told me that was not true, that Nemo is orange, with a large white line and only very small black lines all around. You told me that you would bring Nemo to school the next day for me to see and that's how it was. You brought your stuffed Nemo toy and it was proven that Nemo is orange with a wide white stripe at the base of the head and only very thin black lines around it.

What Does the Story Mean?

Frankie, I was surprised that you remembered to bring the stuffed Nemo toy to school the next day. I realize that you have a good memory and perhaps more importantly, that you keep your word and if you say you are going to do something, you do it. By fulfilling what you said you would do, I realize that you are a responsible child and that I must trust you. Also, you shared with me that you would like to have a Nemo piñata and you asked me if we could buy one at the Target. I told you that maybe we could make the piñata at school. And when you heard me, you said that it was not possible, that you did not think we would go through with it because it would be quite difficult and that you never made a piñata.

Opportunities and Possibilities

Frankie, the conversation we had about a piñata made me think of my own childhood and how excited a piñata would make me feel when I was a child your age. But since my parents didn't have much money, we never bought one and my little brother and I had to learn to make them ourselves with the help of our older cousins. Sometimes, the piñata were made of clay jugs and when they were broken, they made a noise that made us happy because it meant that sweets, fruit, and spare coins would fall soon like a multicolor shower over our heads. So, I promised you we would make a piñata at school. Frankie, you were very happy with the idea! One morning I prepared the pasted at home, which is flour mixed with hot water and used a glue to cover a blown balloon with strips of recycled newspaper. Teacher Sahara brought newspaper from home and teacher Alicia found a large balloon in the closet that we would use as a base to make the piñata in papier mache.

Figure 3.2 Original Learning Story "Francisco, Nemo, and His Piñata!" by Isauro M. Escamilla

A lot of children wanted to help and little by little, the Nemo piñata has been taking shape. A few days later the piñata felt slightly sturdier and teacher Sahara added the fins and tail with cardboard paper. Now, the next thing to do was to decorate it with colorful paper in bright colors. You already know all the colors by heart. I think you will really like to continue working on the elaboration of your Nemo piñata!

Frankie, these photos from December 20, 2019 serve as a reminder of your first classroom-made piñata! You and your friends filled it up with candy and all of you took turns hitting it until it broke and out came all of the treats! Everyone sang the piñata song in Spanish. I hope you carry on with this tradition and when you get older perhaps you will remember how much fun it was to make and break a piñata with your classmates while singing "Dale, dale, dale, no pierdas el tino porque si lo pierdes, pierdes el camino."

Canción de la Piñata (Spanish)

Dale, dale, dale,
No pierdas el tino,
Porque si lo pierdes
Pierdes el camino.
Ya le diste una,
Ya le diste dos,
Ya le diste tres,
Y tu tiempo se acabó.

Piñata Song (English)

Hit it, hit it, hit it,
Don't lose the knack,
Because if you lose it,
You'll lose the way.
You've hit it once,
You've hit it twice,
You've hit is thrice,
Now your time is up.

I think that as a follow-up, perhaps we could try to get the bilingual children's book *La Piñata magica* by Ismael Cala, in which the author encourages the habit of reading in Spanish and English, which will help you improve your skills in both languages. Another book that comes to mind and that you might like is *Hooray: A Piñata* by Elisa Kleven. This book is only in English and I am sure we could find other books related to piñatas in English and/or Spanish at the library.

Frankie, I wonder what your parents think of your interest in the piñata. I think your mom commented that her family is from Peru. In Mexico, the piñata are very common, especially in children's birthdays and December celebrations. I wonder what the traditions of your family in Peru are. Above all I wonder what your mom and dad think about the traditions that we are exploring with you at school.

Frankie, would you like to break the piñatas at school in December or would you like to take it home and save it? By writing this Learning Story I realize how much we need to learn about you and your family!

Opinion of Frankie's Family

How beautiful the tradition of the piñata described in this story! I identify myself in the story and it makes me remember my own childhood since in Peru we also used to celebrate birthdays with piñatas. I have photos with my parents who celebrated my birthday with piñatas from my very first year. My husband also tells me that in Guatemala they celebrate the same way! Piñatas are something fundamental to childhood! Thank you! — Mrs. Ursula, Frankie's mom

The Tradition of Piñatas in Mexico

Did you know that the piñatas arrived in Mexico through the Spanish conquistadores? Although by then, the Maya already used, as a game, to break clay containers filled with cocoa. In Mexico, traditional piñatas are made of clay pots decorated in the form of seven stars peaks. The sweets and fruits that fall when the piñata is broken are the blessings that spill on everyone.

and identity. There is something quite powerful in a group setting with colleagues when you express your hopes for change. For example, when you share with other practitioners your work with young dual language learners or children with a disability, your documentation (reflections, photographs, videos, written stories) reveals firsthand lived experiences from your perspective as an early childhood educator trying to make a difference in the way you teach and learn and the way you are perceived by society. Over time, the focus of our (authors Isauro and Daniel's) inquiry group has evolved to shed light on the development of teaching practices such as observation, documentation, and assessment activities centered on the strengths of children, families, and teachers. In our case, it was up to teachers to insist on having time to reflect on our practices as part of our work to become better educators and feel more productive or efficient and, perhaps more importantly, to be heard and understood. As a result, the inquiry group has afforded us to know one another much better in a semi-formal group setting, and we have become much more aware of who we are both individually and as a team.

In the almost ten years since we brought up to the administration the idea of creating an on-site community of practitioners to discuss issues that matter to us, four administrators have come and gone, but our inquiry group still exists. The current principal supports these teacher-initiated meetings. As a compromise, the principal requested the first half of the meeting be designated to talk about our practice and the second part of the meeting be reserved for district-related topics such as budget, paperwork, and licensing requirements. We think it is a fair compromise and the two instructional coaches assigned to our site by the school district have endorsed the idea of participating and sustaining this community of reflective practitioners to discuss, plan, and act on what we think is the right thing to do on behalf of children, families, and ourselves as early childhood educators.

Chapter Summary

Lessons from the two Learning Stories in this chapter come in great measure from the families' insights shared in their replies to the stories. For example, Genesis's parents state that "disability is not an impediment to show affection and love," while Luna's parents assert that "it goes on to show that this world can be a better place and it all starts when they are little." Luna's mom's hope is for Luna to become a teacher one day but actually, Luna is already teaching us a lesson on acceptance, empathy, and *cariño*, a genuine deep care for someone else, so different and at the same time so similar. All these children, as Genesis's parents say, will go very far in life with the support, empathy, and understanding of people like Luna, with the curiosity and persistence of children like Frankie, and with the open-mindedness of teachers willing to capture stories that touch hearts and minds. These classroom stories invited teachers to think of new ways of observing and creating authentic records of children's learning as a way to understand the meaning behind their ways of being, knowing, and living. In the process, teachers discovered new ways of reflecting, learning, and teaching by writing Learning Stories that reflect who we are both individually and as a community. The two Learning Stories in this chapter focused on children's actual learning that for the most part happens naturally, rather than based on predetermined learning outcomes, moving from the expected and linear to a holistic and at times unpredictable view of children's growth and development. The Learning Stories of Luna, Genesis, and Frankie narratively showcase what children, teachers, and families do, think and hope. These Learning Stories highlight the importance of meaningful curricula driven from children's interests encountered in their everyday play. These Learning Stories place social interactions, relationships, and children's play at the center of early care and education with positive messages to families about their children's lives at school, affirming their identities as competent, inquisitive, and compassionate learners.

Key Points

- The type of observation that predominantly guides Learning Stories are unprompted events that take place at any given time at school. Quite often wonderful things happen throughout the day, since children are constantly discovering something new or making new connections in their interactions with other children, materials, or the environment.
- The use of Learning Stories in early childhood education settings places classroom stories within the broader social context of school communities that work together towards more equitable and inclusive pedagogies.
- Through Learning Stories, teachers engage in pedagogical and intellectual work, humanizing the early childhood profession, moving towards more inclusive modes of observing, analyzing, and understanding the complexities of children's actions and behaviors.
- Children's Learning Stories can create springboards to propel teachers and children to get involved in other class projects and engage with other resources.

References

Bentley, D.F., & M. Souto-Manning. 2019. *Pre-K Stories: Playing with Authorship and Integrating Curriculum in Early Childhood*. New York: Teachers College Press.

Carr, M. 2001. *Assessment in Early Childhood Settings: Learning Stories*. Thousand Oaks, CA: Sage.

Carr, M., & W. Lee. 2012. *Learning Stories: Constructing Learner Identities in Early Education*. Thousand Oaks, CA: Sage.

Carr, M., & W. Lee. 2019. *Learning Stories in Practice*. Thousand Oaks, CA: Sage.

Curtis, D., & M. Carter. 2017. *Learning Together with Young Children: A Curriculum Framework for Reflective Teachers*, 2nd ed.. St. Paul, MN: Redleaf Press.

Hammond, Z. 2014. *Culturally Responsive Teaching and the Brain: Promoting Authentic Engagement and Rigor Among Culturally and Linguistically Diverse Students*. Thousand Oaks, CA: Corwin Press.

Ladson-Billings, G. 2014. "Culturally Relevant Pedagogy 2.0: a.k.a. The Remix." *Harvard Educational Review* 84 (1): 74–84.

Moll, L.C., S. Soto-Santiago, & L. Schwartz. 2013. "Funds of Knowledge in Changing Communities." In *International Handbook of Research on Children's Literacy, Learning, and Culture*, eds. K. Hall, T. Cremin, B. Comber, & L.C. Moll, 172–183. Malden, MA: John Wiley & Sons.

Perry, G., B. Henderson, & D.R. Meier. 2012. *Our Inquiry, Our Practice: Undertaking, Supporting, and Learning from Early Childhood Teacher Research(ers)*. Washington, DC: NAEYC.

4 Integrating Inquiry and Learning Stories for Socialization, Play, and Language

What do we need to add to our practice and our thinking to honor all the complexity of the human beings with whom we spend our days? What are we not looking for, and therefore not seeing?

— Bethica Quinn (2017, 57)

Opening Reflections

- How do Learning Stories help teachers focus on children's strengths with regard to socialization, play, and language learning?
- How do Learning Stories help teachers identify critical moments of children's social and linguistic growth through play
- How does the analysis of Learning Stories that focus on socialization, play, and language deepen teachers' inquiry stance and knowledge?
- How does the integration of Learning Stories in inquiry groups support a professional growth process of focusing on children's socialization, play, and language?

As discussed in earlier chapters, teachers write Learning Stories for the primary purposes of inquiry, assessment, and family engagement in a child's learning. In this chapter we describe how teachers have used Learning Stories for all these purposes, focusing on children's social and emotional development, play and friendships, and multilingual and literacy learning. A Learning Story can serve as both documentation and assessment with regard to a child, a teacher, or an educational activity. Inquiry groups where teachers share their Learning Stories and other forms of documentation can help teachers continue to deepen their thinking about their teaching and their students' learning. Furthermore, teachers can use Learning Stories proactively to engage families in their children's school experiences.

Constructivism and Children's and Teachers' Learning

People learn through constructing and extending their own knowledge, no matter what the content: "All knowing is an action by the knower. Knowledge is brought forth in doing" (Maturana & Varela 1992, 34). Knowledge itself is a construction, and constructivist theory helps describe the biological, social, and cultural genesis of development and learning (Fosnot & Perry 2005). In the classroom, everyone is learning. Children may be learning content (whether cognitive, social, or behavioral), while teachers are learning about children's learning and their own teaching. This learning occurs no matter the context, but inquiry groups can contribute greatly to teachers' targeted development and learning. Further, representing what we learn, and the role of representation in how we learn and how we communicate with one another about what we "know" is integral to building common knowledge together and understanding what and how others "know". Thus, in inquiry groups, teachers construct together further understanding of their classrooms, the children they are teaching, and the families with whom they collaborate in the care for the children, while raising further questions about how to best serve these children, their families, and themselves. These groups provide an arena for both the social and cultural aspects of constructing new understandings for their participants.

One way that inquiry groups can contribute to teachers' construction of knowledge is by providing opportunities for questioning and to experience and acknowledge uncertainty. While these instances may be uncomfortable or challenging, it is through this disequilibrium (the feeling you have when questioning or wondering about what is happening or what to do in a certain situation) that learning and change happen. Questioning your practice and understanding in the context of a supportive group of colleagues can provoke further questioning, disequilibrium, and insights into your teaching, and thus draw on the social and cultural nature of knowledge construction.

Representation and re-representation of ideas through a variety of media support the reflective process essential to the construction of knowledge and understanding and allow for "generalization and re-generalization across experiences, situations and contexts" (Kroll 2018, 304). Telling or writing and illustrating Learning Stories is a prime example of the manifestation of representation. Learning through both telling and hearing Learning Stories requires the construction and reconstruction of essential understandings. Documentation such as Learning Stories can serve as artifacts for reflection and questioning, while consideration of these stories together in inquiry groups can provide further impetus for learning about the child or activity represented in the story, as well as about the teaching that is documented.

Socio-Emotional Development, Play, and Curriculum

One of the most important curricular foci for early childhood teachers is that of social and emotional development, particularly through play. In early childhood centers, children explore how to *learn with* and *relate to* other children in productive ways that will contribute to their abilities to get along in the world. They learn to regulate their own emotions and impulses to learn new things, to focus on that learning, to build friendships with peers, and to interact productively with other people. As discussed above, people learn by constructing their own understandings, given a variety of opportunities to learn. In early childhood centers and schools, teachers aim to provide multiple opportunities for children to construct their understandings of everything they are learning, including how to get along in social interactions and how to regulate their own emotions and impulses.

Expectations for children in kindergarten over the past decade have become much more stringent and academic. The development of self-regulation can provide a resilience in the face of these expectations and a basis for successful learning: "Play and the development of self-regulating behaviors within the context of play can provide children with an opportunity to exercise agency in their own education" (Kroll 2016, 2).

Understanding what children are constructing so as to know what other opportunities to provide can be supported by regular inquiry into your own teaching practice. Learning Stories can provide documentation for reflection on this assessment. Learning Stories also lend themselves to teachers' development of insight and inquiry into their own practices.

> "Documentation is a complex and deep process of teacher research which refers to 'any record of performance that contains sufficient detail to help others understand the behavior recorded'" (Forman & Fyfe 2012, 250, in Kroll 2018, 307).

Play is an integral part of social and emotional development in children and is an important part of the early childhood curriculum in most centers and schools. Through play, children experiment with relationships, friendships, construction, scientific principles, literacy, and mathematical reasoning, among many possibilities. Teachers can tell endless stories about children's play and how that play represents the things children are concerned with and are learning about. An important curriculum for supporting the development of social and emotional development is the provision for play and social interactions around play. Play can be a vehicle for working through issues that are hard to deal with in reality (Kroll 2016), and can be important in helping children develop self-regulation as they learn to navigate the social norms and expectations of school life. While teachers create opportunities for this development, children can also develop those opportunities for themselves.

In one school, two teachers described a game the children had invented called "Help." The children go over to the slide and help one another climb up the ramp. Older children help younger children when the group is made up of mixed ages. However, when it is only the older children (the 4s and 5s), the game is much rougher. Here, children push one another down the slide ramp as well as try to get up the ramp. The teachers commented:

> **In order to play this game without anybody actually getting hurt self-regulation has to happen in three ways: (1) to control their actual bodies so that although they might be crashing into somebody, they're crashing into them with a certain amount of gentleness, but there's also (2) a certain amount of self-regulation (*of emotional response*), someone just smashed their foot into my face, but this is a game, and this is part of the game and I'm not gonna fall apart because of it; . . . (3) the other side of it is the same thing, that the kids who would slip into anger really easily who have to stop themselves when somebody smashes into them . . . and it's especially clear in this game. . . you could see them take that moment to think about whether they were going to have their usual response (*having a tantrum, falling apart*) and then make a conscious decision not to because they wanted to be able to stay in the game. (Kroll 2017, 866)**

In this scenario, children have created an opportunity to practice self-regulation within rough and tumble play in a safe environment, where the children can make their own decisions about how they want to interact and play, and the teachers view it as an opportunity for children to learn different ways to play together—caring for one another when they are "helping" one another and practicing regulated rough and tumble play and self-control as well. The teacher who described this scenario went on to comment on what and how 4-year-olds learn:

> **She observed that because being four is about understanding how to get along with other people, then play becomes the vehicle for working that out. It is as if the children are thinking or saying: "*It's almost as if we (the 4-year-olds) have to figure out how to get along with each other because that's what being 4 years old is all about. So what are we going to do, well let's play, and then we'll see what happens while we play and we'll get into a conflict and we'll solve it*". . . . It seems as if the drive to play comes out of the need to learn to be together. (Kroll 2017, 867).**

Thus, in this extended example, you can see how social development and play interact so powerfully with one another.

While the teacher did not write a Learning Story about this interaction, it would make a wonderful Learning Story to discuss the development of children's play, social relations, and self-regulation.

KEY IDEA

Play

DeVries et al. (2002) point out that how children play and what children play changes as they develop: "Evolution in forms of play reflects developmental advances that should be valued. Play is useful to children as they try to understand the world in which they live. Piaget, Dewey, and Vygotsky provide educators with a strong rationale for the value of play and work in early education, and to appreciate how work can evolve from play" (10).

Learning Stories About Social and Emotional Learning

One of the Learning Stories featured in Chapter 3 highlights social and emotional learning and development. The Learning Story about the development of Genesis and Luna's friendship demonstrates children's tendencies to accept one another for who they are and to play together with great joy.

In writing Learning Stories, teachers practice inquiry and documentation. As teachers learn to write such stories, they are also learning a way of documenting their teaching and inquiring into children's learning and their own understanding of that learning. I (author Linda Kroll) have been working with a group of teachers in an independent preschool for the past two years. They have been experimenting with different ways of documenting their inquiry questions. When I introduced Learning Stories to them, they were eager to experiment with this methodology. One of the first Learning Stories was written by Teacher Aaron to his small group of 3-year-olds. Many of the children were in their first year of preschool and were learning what it was like to be with many children for a certain amount of time every day. Aaron's group had six children. During small group time, he developed a curriculum around the children acting out conflicts using toy animals and making suggestions for solutions. In documenting this activity, he wrote a letter to his group. This letter was his first attempt at writing a Learning Story to his group of students, who call themselves the Cookies.

> Dear Cookies,
>
> "What is a friend?"
>
> I have been watching and listening to you all at our group time, and I see that you have some good ideas about what a friend is. I also see that this is a question we might not all have the answer to.
>
> At group time I have asked, "What makes a friend?" You have had some good answers like, "playing together," "taking care of each other," "reading a book with someone" and "I don't know." I have asked, "What can you say to friends when you want to play with them?" You answered, "Let's play a picnic," "I want to play with you," "I said let's go play Evie," "Let's go play in the sand Felix," "Let's Go!," "Let's Play!," and "I don't know." When I asked, "How can you be a friend?" You answered, "You love them and care for them", "I take care of June, playing babies. June is the Dad, I'm the Mom.", "By playing!" "I always play picnic.", and "I don't know yet." These are all good answers. Maybe we need practice? Maybe we need time to practice being friends and making friends? One thing I know for certain is, I love being your teacher, and I love watching the ways you are working hard and practicing at being friends and being kind and respectful.
>
> Sometimes at group time our animal friends come out because they need our help to solve their problems. Teacher Bear, Hippie, Ellie, Pandy, and Piggie all love it when the Cookies help to solve problems. One day Piggie was feeling very sad about being at school. Piggie was crying and rolling around so frustrated because they just wanted to go home. None of the animals knew how to help, even Teacher Bear didn't

know what to do. When Teacher Bear asked the Cookies if they had any ideas, guess what happened? The Cookies went to the Room 5 comfort photo box and started collecting comfort photos then gave the comfort photos to Piggie and told Piggie that they hoped Piggie felt better soon. It worked! I was so proud of you Cookies for knowing how to help, and having ideas, and practicing acts of kindness.

We don't have all the answers about what a friend is or how to be a friend yet, but we'll keep searching for and practicing ideas and ways that we can be friends.

I love you Cookies! I'm very proud of you.

Love, your friend,

Aaron

In this letter, Aaron reflected on what the children have been doing ("What is the story?"), on what it meant, and on what comes next, although he did not label each part as such. He also described the problem or question they were seeking to explore—"What makes a friend?" When he read the story to the group, the discussion that followed focused on the crucial question of how children develop friendships and learn to be a friend. This question is one of those at the heart of social and emotional curricula. The topic of learning to be together as friends appeared also in other Learning Stories written by other teachers in this discussion group. In the discussion that followed Aaron's sharing of his Learning Story, the teachers commented on how children in this group were displaying acts of kindness and friendship in other contexts in the classroom, such as during choice time and outside time. They noted the development of new friendships and problem solving that were occurring in many different contexts. Teachers Laura and Ayla were both inspired to create their own Learning Stories about the development of friendships and mutual support among children. For example, Teacher Ayla's Learning Story discussed in Chapter 1 came after Teacher Aaron's; it has a wonderful example of children supporting one another's learning with the mantra "practice makes better." (Rather than "practice makes perfect," which could be very discouraging to a struggling learner).

More Story Insights

Aaron's Learning Story shows examples of children developing language around how to discuss issues of friendship, kindness and play negotiation, as well as how to solve emotional dilemmas such as feeling sad or lonely.

The work accomplished together in the inquiry group sparked an investigation into how the children in this classroom are learning to make friends, to negotiate with friends, to play with friends, and to support one another as fellow learners. While the construction of friendship and peer relationships is already a central curricular area in early childhood education, the creation of Learning Stories around this theme highlighted for these three teachers what was happening in their classroom with their young students that both demonstrated the occurrence of this development and raised questions about what other ways they could support this learning among their children. Not unimportantly, this conversation and reflection also helped deepen the teachers' collaboration and friendship with one another—so that the construction of social relationships continued with both children and teachers. The next step for them was thinking about how to include parents and families in this process.

Thus, constructivist theory helps teachers to interpret and understand what and how they can learn from writing Learning Stories and sharing them with one another in inquiry groups. As teachers question one another's stories and reflect back to each other what they have heard and learned from each other, Learning Stories can provide a link between children's construction of knowledge and about their teaching and their classrooms. Writing a Learning Story provides a teacher with a structured opportunity to reflect on what they have observed and done in their classrooms with regard to a particular child and their actions and responses. While writing, they can construct and reconstruct their understanding of the particulars of the Learning Story and reflect on their understandings of children's learning and their own teaching. In the process of sharing Learning Stories, teachers can challenge one another's interpretations, causing some disequilibrium for both the writer and the responders, which can lead to further construction of their understandings and to further questions.

KEY IDEA

Constructing Social Relationships

In *Moral Classrooms, Moral Children* (DeVries & Zan 1994), Rheta DeVries points out that pleasurable shared experiences promote sociomoral development: "When children experience special friendships and the satisfaction of playing with others, they are motivated to prevent and work out conflicts" (210).

Learning Stories on Socialization, Play, and Language: The Benefits of Inquiry Groups

When Learning Stories focusing on socialization, play, and language are featured in inquiry groups, teachers are afforded a professional space and forum to document and share the small moments of children's growth and their learning over time. Ongoing inquiry group meetings allow educators to deepen and broaden their understanding of children's socialization, play, and language learning over weeks, months, and even years.

For instance, during one meeting of the Las Americas inquiry group, Mary Lin (Cantonese/English dual language head teacher) noted that Learning Stories about children's play and socialization "help us get to know children in a more personal way. It's a more relaxed form of observation and learning for us." At the same meeting, Penelope Ho (Cantonese/English dual language instructional coach) presented her Learning Story entitled, "What About Me?" that explored one child's social growth. Penelope explained her reasoning for choosing this child: "I have observed this child all year long, and I intentionally wanted to see how she was doing socially toward the end of the school year."

Writing a Learning Story on play and socialization provides an opportunity for teachers to see and reflect on how children might be feeling as they learn to make new friends and learn through play. Observing a child engage with a new playmate or become excited by a new game, triggers feelings in the teachers. Sharing these feelings in Learning Stories creates a more complete and nuanced picture of the child for everyone to see and from which everyone can learn. For example, Erin, the head teacher in the Las Americas special education classroom said, "We have to do a lot of IEPs (Individualized Educational Plans), and they are dry writing. But when I create these Learning Stories about children's play and social growth, I get to share my feelings." When Erin listened to Lauren Boyles, the Spanish/English dual language coach in the inquiry group, read her Learning Story in the meeting about two of Erin's children, Erin remarked, "It's beautiful to see this Learning Story about my children. I get to see their learning in a new way, to see their progress and growth. I'm excited to share it with Jazmin's family."

The entire inquiry group also benefits from an emotional connection to Learning Stories that focus on the challenges and triumphs of children's socialization, play, and language learning. For instance, I (author Isauro) often share with the group how certain Learning Stories affect me emotionally and connect me to the group, the children, and their families I often have emotional connections to the stories. I feel a sense of ownership. But the Learning Story belongs to everyone, to the children, to the families, and the teachers. When people feel these emotions, we have powerful interactions. How does it feel to hold a deeply personal Learning Story in your hands? The powerful emotions often shown in Learning Stories about children's efforts to make friends or to find the best words to initiate play make for stories that touch everyone, and in this communal process of the inquiry group these Learning Stories become "owned" by the group.

The sharing of photographs of children at play and socializing with peers also helps teachers capture a moment or series of moments that give insight into children's actions and nonverbal communication. For example, Mary Lin notes, "When I take photographs of children's social interaction and play, I get in tune with the moment, and then later I remember more about what happened when I revisit the photographs."

The creation and sharing of Learning Stories about social interaction, play, and language also encourage inquiry group members to take on the perspectives of the children featured in a Learning Story. For example, Lauren Boyles created another Learning Story, "Cooking for Thomas," in which she told the story of Jazmin and Thomas playing together in the kitchen area one afternoon. Both children attended Las Americas' special education classroom. Here's how Lauren started the Learning Story:

> Jazmin, at free playtime in the afternoon, you and Thomas were playing in the kitchen area together. Thomas sat at the table while you sat at the toy stove. You brought him a plate with some bread on it, and Thomas pushed it away saying "yucky." You took that plate away and brought him a new plate, with beans on it. You looked at him while he put the fork on the beans. You verbalized and then brought the bread on the plate to the other seat, brought cups and two spoons, and sat down with Thomas to "eat."

When Lauren presented this Learning Story to the inquiry group, she said that she had decided to tell the story through Jazmin's perspective, but that she could also have told it through Thomas' perspective. Lauren decided to write the Learning Story through Jazmin's perspective because she wanted to highlight Jazmin's actions in the play interaction as evidence of her growth in this area. Lauren wrote about Jazmin's growth in the "What Does it Mean?" section of the Learning Story:

> You are able to communicate and collaborate so much with Thomas! You're engaging in pretend play and in collaborative play, which are both important developmental milestones. You follow the cues of your friends, watching Thomas to see what he would think of his new plate of food, and responding accordingly with patience to his "picky" eating. Without exchanging any words, you and Thomas were able to engage in this scene together right until clean up time. I wonder how much longer it would have gone on for!

Choosing to tell the Learning Story of the play partners from Jazmin's perspective allows Lauren to pinpoint specific elements of Jazmin's pretend and collaborative play and to show how Jazmin can intuit the underlying meaning of play partners' actions.

More Story Insights

This interaction between Jazmin and Thomas is a good example of self-regulation and cooperation in play. When Thomas rejects the bread as "yucky," Jazmin could have reacted with anger or disappointment. Instead, she is paying attention to her play partner's desires and needs and is choosing to continue the play by including Thomas's perspective in their play together. All this occurs without much language, but with much representational interaction.

The sharing of Learning Stories that capture children's achievements in play, socialization, and language also promotes rich new ideas from group participants about possible next steps to support a child. For instance, I (author Isauro) wrote a story about 4-year-old Aleksey, who was learning to walk on "stilts" (two overturned plastic buckets attached to rope) on the school playground. After I presented this story of Aleksey's determination and skill in stilt walking, a group member suggested that I take Aleksey to the park down the street as another environment for Aleksey's stilt walking and for other game opportunities where he would challenge himself by walking on a tightrope or climbing up the rope pyramid play structure. This suggestion was recorded in the meeting minutes; at the next inquiry group meeting, we revisited this suggestion, and my coteachers and I shared a brief video and photographs that documented the field trip to the park with Aleksey and the entire preschool class.

When multiple Learning Stories are presented in an inquiry group session, and as Learning Stories accumulate over the course of months and years, group members are afforded a valuable professional opportunity to reflect on the varied developmental trajectories of individual children, and to see how children's learning changes over time. For instance, at one meeting of the Las Americas inquiry group, the group members presented a total of six Learning Stories—five stories were presented by regular group members and one by a visiting infant/toddler teacher, Azul Muller, from a nearby center:

- Learning Story #1: "One, Two, Three Steps Closer" by Azul Muller
- Learning Story #2: "My First Day of Preschool" by Alicia Alvarez
- Learning Story #3: "Nathan, the Football Soccer Player" by Isauro M. Escamilla
- Learning Story #4: "Girls Building Blocks" by Mary Lin
- Learning Story #5: "Angela Planting a Flower" by Joanne Yu
- Learning Story #6: "Hazel, A Teacher in the Making" by Edwin Serrano

1. Azul's "One, Two, Three Steps Closer" told the story, written in both Spanish and English, of helping 13-month-old Gael take a few steps in the classroom (this Learning Story is described in more detail later in this chapter).
2. In Alicia's "My First Day of School,“ Alicia wrote about Nathan's first day at preschool, his challenges in interacting with friends as he learns to speak and converse, and his attempt to play with another child, Luna (this Learning Story is also described in more detail later in this chapter).
3. My (author Isauro's) Learning Story "Nathan, the Football Soccer Player," written just a week after Alicia wrote her story to Nathan ("My First Day of Preschool“), illustrates how Nathan became more comfortable in his new preschool environment and I realized his tremendous joy in playing soccer with other children.

> Nathan, I see that you have a real disposition for sports. You like to participate in different activities when we go out to play in the school playground. More than anything else, you enjoy playing soccer football. You have much more strength than I imagined, and you coordinate your movements quite well. I am surprised that you are able to calculate the distance you should be from the ball to hit with the necessary strength to reach where you want to send it.

4. Mary's Learning Story, "Girls Building Blocks," describes a small group of girls who loved to build with Legos and blocks. Mary explained that she asked the girls what they were doing and observed their play for 50 minutes. Cynthia Romero, the teaching assistant in the special education classroom across the playground was also observing at the time, as one of her children was included in the children's play that morning in the classroom. Mary took written notes, photographs, and documented the children's building, and used this data for her DRDP assessments on the children. After Mary read her Learning Story out loud in the meeting, I (author Isauro) wondered whether Mary might make one child more of a protagonist in the story so that the parents could respond more directly to that child. The group also offered suggestions for next steps such as having the children draw pictures based on their block constructions, and Mary thought she could add a "Possibilities" section to the Learning Story and ask the parents for a response.

5. Before reading her Learning Story, "Angela Planting a Flower," to the group, Joanne explained that the story was about 3-year-old Angela's interest in planting a flower. Joanne had read a big book called *Seed*, and asked the children if anyone wanted to plant a seed. Angela and a few others agreed. Joanne read the Learning Story, written in Cantonese and English, in English to the group and said some words in Cantonese. The story described Joanne and Angela's conversation in English and Cantonese as they counted and planted the seeds. Joanne noted that Angela learned new English vocabulary, and Angela's mother responded to the Learning Story in English. Joanne wrote that Angela wanted to practice her English and is helpful at home with planting. Angela and her mother bought a flower from the grocery store and water it once a week. Angela's mom responded that she wanted Angela to increase her responsibility and check the flower daily. Angela also responded to her mother's message, which she dictated to Joanne in Chinese: "I like flowers. My sister likes flowers too. My mom buys flowers from Safeway. I helped my mom to water the plant at home." Joanne also added DRDP assessment measures to the Learning Story to indicate Angela's understanding of certain language and social elements.

6. In Edwin's in-progress Learning Story, "Hazel, A Teacher in the Making," Edwin wrote about Hazel (the oldest child in the class) teaching a small group of five peers using a dry erase board. Edwin observed that Hazel wrote letters and numbers on the board and had the children repeat these back to her. Hazel also asked, "Who wants a chance to write on the board?", and Hazel told the children if their writing was correct or not. All the children waited for their turn. Hazel said, "/ppppp/ for a p letter." Hazel was correct in her letter and numeral writing except for reversing the number 2; another child said, "That's not how you write it." Hazel said, "Ok, let's do another one." Edwin highlighted how this Learning Story showcases Hazel's knowledge of certain sounds and letters and numbers, and her knowledge of how to ask questions and invite others to participate. Edwin noted that he will add new sections in the more complete draft of this Learning Story.

The presentation, sharing, and reflection on the six Learning Stories made for a lively meeting focused on stories of several children learning to talk, socialize, build, create, read, and write in multiple languages with peers and adults. The Learning Stories helped the group see how the children's learning in these areas is embedded in children's interests, desires, and needs. In this sense, it helps to show teachers not only what children are capable of learning in these developmental areas, but also how important it is for teachers to support children's initiative and agency in this process. For example, Azul's story about Gael taking a few steps in the classroom highlights the intense desire of a young child learning to walk. The Learning Stories also helped the group see and feel the challenges that all children experience at some point in their development and learning. For instance, Alicia's "My First Day of School" shows how some 3-year-olds are just at the beginning stages of learning to speak and interact with peers. My (author Isauro's) story, "Nathan, the Football Soccer Player," indicates the importance of recognizing children's play talents—"Nathan, playing soccer football requires you to be a team player, collaborate with others and learn to share."

KEY IDEA

Supporting Interests and Initiative

The Learning Stories helped the group see how the children's learning in these areas is embedded in children's interests, desires, and needs. In this sense, it helps to show teachers not only what children are capable of learning in these developmental areas, but also how important it is for teachers to support children's initiative and agency in this process.

The Learning Stories from this one meeting also provide a snapshot of children's development. In terms of constructivist and socio-constructivist theory (Vygostky 1978), these stories reveal children's efforts to construct their own learning (e.g., the girls building with blocks, Angela planting seeds with Joanne) within social, intellectual, and linguistic routines in the classroom. The stories show how the children use play as a primary vehicle for discovery and creation, and then add layers of multilingualism to deepen their connections with peers and adults and to share their learning with others. Children's social constructivist learning is tied fundamentally to their desires and to playful discovery, as Vygotsky (1978) explains:

> But ignore the child's needs, and the incentives which are effective in getting him to ask, we will never be able to understand in advance from one developmental stage to the next, because every advance is connected with a marked change and motives, inclinations, and incentives (92).
>
> . . . [The] preschool child enters an imaginary, illusory world which the unreliable desires can be realized, and we call this world play. Imagination is a new psychological process for the child . . . . Like all functions of consciousness, it originally arises from action (93).

The stories also show the development and evolution of schema (Curtis & Jaboneta 2019; Piaget & Inhelder 2000) that provide children with intellectual and physical parameters or throughlines for playful creations and discoveries, as seen in Hazel's use of the familiar schema or structure of playing "school" and Angela's understanding of what it takes to grow flowers both at home and school. While the group's Learning Stories did not use this kind of academic or research language, this was essentially what the group was exposed to and reflected on over the course of the 90-minute meeting.

Learning Stories Across a Developmental Continuum

The following Learning Stories, which are arranged from the youngest to the oldest children, highlight the varied developmental considerations and profiles that Learning Stories can illuminate in terms of children's social-emotional, physical, and linguistic growth.

Azul's Learning Story for Gael: "One, Two, Three Steps Closer"

Azul Muller presented her Learning Story, "One, Two, Three Steps Closer," which chronicles thirteen-month-old Gael's early attempts to walk (Figure 4.1).

Azul prefaced her Learning Story by explaining that Gael was becoming the first walker in the classroom because of Azul's support and Gael's overall "perseverance and determination." Azul shared Gael's Learning Story with his mother, who asked, "Why doesn't he show me he's walking?" Azul shared the photo of Gael walking to his mother on the Monday after it happened on a Friday. Azul then sent more photographs to Gael's mother, who wanted to share them on Facebook. Because Azul's Learning Story documented Gael's first time walking in the classroom, I (author Isauro) remarked to the group that we could call it a "first-time story." Azul told us that she planned to print out the Learning Story on larger paper and display several copies on the classroom walls.

Azul's story shows that learning to walk is also a social and community activity and pursuit. Azul's photographs show the close proximity of Kayla (Azul's coteacher who was with Gael) and Gael, and yet they also show how Kayla is actually not touching Gael, but has positioned her body low to the ground, with arms and hands outstretched to support Gael's efforts. Azul is the focus of Gael's walking, as he tries to reach her. Kayla's physical presence is not so much to catch Gael if he falls, but to signal to Gael that she is there with him, for him, and trusts that even if he falls, he will get back up and try again as he wishes. In this sense, Kayla provides support for Gael that is as much social and emotional as physical. It is also cultural and communal, as Azul displays culturally relevant and supportive actions and language ("Hi Gael, I missed you. Do you want to sit with me? Come over.") and has written the Learning Story in Spanish first, Gael's home language and the medium for Azul's initial "conversation" with Gael. In writing the story first in Spanish, Azul honors the language that Gael and his mother share, and also the use of Spanish in Gael's classroom.

One, Two, Three Steps Closer

Azul Muller
March 15, 2019

What's Happening?

Dear Gael,

In the afternoon I was sitting at the desk doing some paperwork. I was not in the classroom all day and Kayla was with you today. When you noticed me, you crawled out of the play area and you then stood up on your own holding your balance in the middle of the walkway. Kayla came on over and kneeled right behind you. I said, "Hi Gael, I missed you!" I held my arms wide open and you took a step forward and fell. You giggled on your way down. I said, "Gael, do you want to sit with me? Come over." I then got my phone, and you were so excited. You held your arms open and kept your balance. You looked down then back up and there it was, one, two, three steps closer. You fell again and that didn't stop you. You got up and into my arms you were.

Sincerely,
Azul

What Does It Mean?

Gael, you filled me with joy when I saw you take your first steps in the classroom. Your mom shared with me that during the weekend you were taking some of your first steps. I was waiting patiently this week, watching you carefully trying to capture your special moment to share with mom. Alicia F. Liberman, articulates that babies and young children thrive when they feel secure in their parents' care as they experiment with their bodies, relationships, and physical environment. I can see that you also feel safe and secure in our classroom. You were also patient, you made sure you were balanced before you took some steps. As you continue to explore your space, I hope to continue to provide you with a secure, positive and challenging environment that will help you grow.

Opportunities and Possibilities

Gael, you have shown me your first steps and I am excited to see what else you will show me. Now that I see you walking, I wonder how can we continue to challenge and provide you an environment for exploration. We as a classroom want to ensure we continue to provide you with a safe and nurturing environment. You are our first walker in the classroom, and I can't wait to see what the other children will learn from you. Your patience, stability, and persistence are some of the many strengths you showed us today.

Allowing space to explore their environment through large movement, children will learn they are strong, confident, and safe in any physical pursuit.

-Angela J. Hanscom

DRDP Measures Infant/Toddler

1. ATL-REG 1: Attention Maintenance
2. ATL-REG 2: Self-Comforting
3. ATL-REG 5: Self-Control of Feelings and Behavior
4. SED 1: Identity of Self in Relation to Others
5. SED 3: Relationships and Social Interactions with Familiar Adults
6. PD-HLTH 1: Perceptual-Motor Skills and Movement Concepts
7. PD-HLTH 2: Gross Locomotor Movement Skills
8. PD-HLTH 3: Gross Motor Manipulative Skills

Figure 4.1 Original Learning Story "One, Two, Three Steps Closer," by Azul Muller

Uno, Dos, Tres Pasos Mas Cerca

¿Qué Está Pasando?

Querido Gael,

Por la tarde estaba sentada en el escritorio haciendo unos papeles. No estuve en el aula todo el día y Kayla estuvo contigo hoy. Cuando me notaste, te arrastraste fuera del área de juego y luego te levantaste, manteniendo el equilibrio en medio del camino. Kayla se acercó y se arrodilló justo detrás de ti. Te dije: "Hola Gael, ¡te eché de menos!" mantuve mis brazos abiertos de par en par y diste un paso adelante y caíste. Te reías mientras bajabas. Te dije: "Gael, ¿quieres sentarte conmigo? Pasa." Entonces conseguí mi cámara y estabas tan emocionado. mantuviste los brazos abiertos y el equilibrio mirando hacia abajo, y luego hacia arriba y allí estabas uno, dos, tres pasos más cerca. Te caiste de nuevo y eso no te detuvo. Te levantaste y en mis brazos estabas.

Sinceramente,
Azul

¿Qué Significa?

Gael, me llenaste de alegría cuando te vi dar tus primeros pasos en el aula. Tu madre me contó que durante el fin de semana estabas dando algunos de tus primeros pasos. Estuve esperando pacientemente esta semana, observándote cuidadosamente intentando capturar tu momento especial para compartir con mamá. Alicia F. Liberman, expresa que los bebés y los niños pequeños prosperan cuando se sienten seguros al cuidado de sus padres al experimentar con sus cuerpos, relaciones y entorno físico. Puedo ver que también te sientes seguro en nuestro salón. También fuiste paciente, te aseguraste de estar equilibrado antes de dar algunos pasos. A medida que continúes explorando tu espacio, espero continuar brindándote un entorno seguro, positivo y desfiante que te ayudará a crecer.

Oportunidades

Gael, me has mostrado tus primeros pasos y estoy emocionada de ver qué más me mostrarás. Ahora que te veo caminando, me pregunto cómo podemos continuar ofreciendote retos y brindándote un entorno para la exploración. Eres nuestro primer caminante en el aula, no puedo esperar a ver qué aprenderán de ti los demás niños.

Al permitir espacio para explorar su entorno a través de grandes movimientos, los niños aprenderán que son fuertes y seguros en cualquier actividad física.

-Angela J. Hanscom

Figure 4.1 Original Learning Story "One, Two, Three Steps Closer," by Azul Muller

Alicia's Learning Story for Nathan: "My First Day of Preschool"

Alicia Alvarez's Learning Story documents the first day of school for Nathan, aged 2.9 at the time of the Learning Story (Figure 4.2).

> **More Story Insights**
>
> In this story it is interesting to note the combination of physical, emotional, and social development that support Gael's learning to walk. It is *within a social and cultural context* that Gael is practicing walking and persisting in his efforts. The social support provided by the two adults (Kayla and Azul) is a lovely example of how children and teachers support each other in the child's learning. Gael's delight is matched by his teachers' support and delight.

Alicia wrote the Learning Story in early July and then I (author Isauro) translated it into English for our first Las Americas inquiry group meeting in September, where she presented it. Alicia selected several photographs from the array of photos that she took on Nathan's first day in school. The photographs tell their own story of Nathan's emotions, actions, and overtures at friendship and play on his first day of school. The photographs in Figure 4.3 are a selection from the original learning story. They depict the range of Nathan's emotions and actions from a close physical connection with his father, Carlos (photo 2) to his playful interactions with Luna (photo 9) to Nathan's solo play on the slide and with the ball (photos 5 and 7). The photographs show the social, emotional, friendship, and physical transition that Nathan made that morning on his first day of school. Along with Nathan, many children experience such emotions at a young age when entering a formal school setting. The photographs, without words, also depict the actions of adults (Carlos, his father) and peers (Luna, a new friend) as well as the "hidden" actions of Alicia, an observant teacher inquirer and careful documenter. When you read and look at the finished Learning Story, you see the powerful communal and culturally supportive roles that Carlos, Luna, and Alicia played in understanding and supporting Nathan's transition.

In the first section of the Learning Story, Alicia started her story to Nathan in the present tense, an effective technique for helping readers go back in time to Nathan's first day and to help relive and re-experience that day along with Nathan, Alicia, Carlos, and Susana (his mother).

> **What Did I Observe?**
>
> Nathan, today is your first day in preschool. I understand how it is difficult for you to separate from your dad. I see it in your eyes, but I want to tell you that we are going to do everything possible to make you feel safe and comfortable in this new stage of your life. Let's help you make new friends, learn new games, and new songs. You'll learn by playing, and you'll see how much fun it is. It is a great pleasure to have you in our classroom, and I want to welcome you!

Based on what she observed and felt, Alicia indicated her own emotions and level of empathy ("I understand how it is difficult for you to separate from your dad. I see it in your eyes") and "tells" Nathan that the teachers will help Nathan "make new friends, learn new games, and new songs." Although Alicia wrote the Learning Story after Nathan's first day, she provided readers with a direction and plan for supporting Nathan's social, emotional, and playful entry into the school and his gradual transition to feeling comfortable and accepted beyond the first day.

Mi Primer Día en Preescolar

Alicia Álvarez
Julio 2 2018

¿Qué Observé?

Nathan hoy es tu primer día en preescolar. Entiendo que es muy difícil para ti la separación con tu papá. Lo veo en tus ojitos pero te quiero decir que nosotros vamos hacer todo posible para que te sientas seguro y confortable en está nueva etapa de tu vida.

Vamos a ayudarte hacer nuevos amigos, aprender nuevos juegos, y canciones. Vas a aprender jugando; ya verás que divertido es. Es un gran placer tenerte en nuestro salón y quiero darte la bienvenida.

¿Qué Aprendizaje Veo?

Nathan veo que pronto hiciste una buena amistad con Luna. A pesar que no hablaste mucho Luna logró hacerte sentir mejor después que se fue tu papá. Nathan, tú demostraste que eres muy amistoso y te gusta compartir y tomar turnos al compartir con Luna los juguetes. Y cuando salimos al jardín seguiste jugando con ella y te veías muy feliz.

Oportunidades y Posibilidades

Tratar de hacer cada día más fácil la separación. Ofrecerle los juguetes que le gustan y con la ayuda de Luna, tratar de que se sienta seguro y confortable. Jugar pelota con él y correr; ya que demostró que jugar pelota es su juego preferido.

¿Qué Opinan los Padres de Nathan?

Nathan, sé que es tu primer día en preescolar. Tanto a ti como a nosotros tus papás nos dolió separarnos, pero así tiene que ser tarde o temprano. Pero cuando tu papá me dijo que Luna te ayudó a sentirte mejor me dio gusto. No sabia que Luna estaba en el mismo salón. Luna es una niña hermosa y amistosa que conocí desde bebé y después, cuando naciste tú, ella te conoció; pero ya tenía tiempo que no la mirábamos. Ojalá y su amistad siga y con el tiempo puedas convivir con tus demás compañeros. Sé que eres un niño amistoso pero como aún no puedes hablar bien, te cuesta entenderte con otros niños; y más por el idioma Inglés. Pero sé que hice bien en inscribirte en el preescolar para que aprendas a hablar tanto Español como Inglés y así puedas convivir con tus compañeritos y otros niños que conozcas en algún parque. Y también aprendas muchas otras cosas más como a cantar, colorear, contar números, leer, escribir, etc.

— Mamá

Figure 4.2 Original Learning Story "My First Day of Preschool," by Alicia Alvarez

Figure 4.3 Photos from "My First Day of Preschool"

In the next section, Alicia described the quick social contact between Nathan and Luna, which was initiated by Luna.

> **What Learning Do I See?**
>
> Nathan, I see that you found a good friend in Luna. Even though you did not talk much, Luna managed to make you feel better after your dad left. Nathan, you showed that you are very friendly, and you like to share and take turns playing with Luna. When we went out to the garden you kept playing with her, and you looked very happy.

Luna has a particular affinity for initiating social contact, play, and interactions with other children. Alicia also narrated the children's playful encounter by taking into account Nathan's perspective ("Nathan, you showed that you are very friendly, and you like to share and take turns playing with Luna") and Luna's ("Luna managed to make you feel better after your dad left") in the same section of the Learning Story. Alicia then added ideas for making Nathan's school days easier.

> **Opportunities and Possibilities**
>
> To try to make the separation from his dad easier every day, we will offer him the toys he likes and with Luna's help we'll try to make him feel safe and comfortable. We'll play with the ball and run since it seems that playing ball is his favorite game.

Susana, Nathan's mother, noted in her comments (originally written by hand in Spanish) about how Luna befriended Nathan.

> **What Do Nathan's Parents Think?**
>
> Nathan, I know it's your first day in preschool. The separation was as hard for us, your parents as it was for you, but this was supposed to happen sooner or later. But when your dad told me that Luna helped you feel better, I felt better too. I did not know that Luna was in the same classroom. Luna is a beautiful and friendly little girl that I've known since she was a baby. And when you were born, she got to know you too. It has been quite a while since the last time we saw Luna. Hopefully, you and she will become friends and as time goes by, you will make new friends. I know that you are a friendly little boy but since you cannot speak well yet, it is hard for you to understand other children; and even more in the English language. But I know that enrolling you in preschool was the right thing to do so that you can learn to speak both Spanish and English and be able to interact with your classmates and other children you might meet at the park. And you'll also learn many other things like singing, coloring, counting numbers, reading, writing, etc. — Mom

Susana's response allowed her to express her own feelings of empathy and sharing in the emotional challenge of the day for Nathan, Carlos, and herself ("The separation was as hard for us, your parents, as it was for you").

More Story Insights

The first day of school is significant for all children. In this Learning Story, you see Nathan's attachment to his father and his resilience in finding a friend to help with the separation transition. Starting school is a developmental milestone for every child; having teachers, other children, and parents who are supportive and empathetic help the child to co-regulate and self-regulate in this potentially stressful context.

Ellie's Learning Story: "種植 Planting"

During the COVID-19 health crisis, the Las Americas inquiry group met online, and the teachers only saw the children in distance learning. Joanne Yu decided to continue her writing of Learning Stories with her 3-year-old niece, Ellie, with whom she spent time during the COVID-19 pandemic (Figure 4.4).

Joanne and Ellie planted together in Joanne's backyard, which offered Joanne the opportunity to observe Ellie's interactions, language, and playful actions with the plant materials, with the tools, and with Joanne. Joanne and Ellie spoke entirely in Cantonese, and Joanne wrote the Learning Story in Cantonese first, and then translated it into English to share with the Las Americas inquiry group via email.

In this Learning Story, Joanne's photographs capture at almost ground level Ellie's construction of the flower planting process, from shoveling the dirt to adding decorative rocks to watering the succulent in the pot. For the "What Happened?" section of the Learning Story, Joanne wrote:

> 發生的事情：瞳瞳,今天早上當你看見我種花後，你問我："我可不可以種花花？"我說可以.於是你拿起鏟子鏟起泥土，放在花盆内.你說: "我自己能做，不用你幫." 我說: "很好,你很独立." 然後，你問我: "這花花放在哪裡?".我教你怎樣把花種入泥內，你把花種入泥內後，然後用裝飾石頭放在泥土上,最後用花洒澆水.
>
> **What Happened?:** You saw me planting flowers and wanted to try it this morning, so you shoveled the dirt into the flowerpot. You said you were able to do it with no help. I said, "That's good, you're very independent." And then you asked me, "Where does the flower go?" I taught you how to plant the flower within the dirt. After you put the flower into the dirt, and then you placed decorative rocks on the top, finally you watered it.

This section of the Learning Story indicates Joanne's balancing of independent and co-constructed social skills and knowledge, and indicates a cultural and familial value underlying their interaction of competence and independence.

In the "What Does It Mean?" section, Joanne extended and deepened her reflections on the social, play, and linguistic value of the Learning Story by noting that "children have the tendency to change their minds about doing an activity after they have seen someone else do it." Joanne effectively moved from the particular of Ellie, her niece, to other children with whom she has worked, making an important connection about the value of balancing independent and socially-constructed action and play.

> 這意味着什麼：在後花园，瞳瞳開始只想玩水，不想跟我種花，當我種完花後，叫她浇水，她很樂意，浇完水後, 瞳瞳問我："我可不可以種花花？"小孩子有時是這樣，當有機會看到你做的東西後，覺得有興趣，就有可能改變主意，想做她原來不想做的東西.她只有三歲半，能運用整句句子來問，說明她有好的語言能力. 她說她自己能用鏟子鏟泥，不用我幫，她把泥裝在盆内，這説明她有表達自己想法的能力.然後她學我那樣，將植物種入盆內，把小石頭壓住泥土.這說明她有模仿能力.
>
> **What Does This Mean?:** When we first started going out into the backyard, she only wanted to play with water. She didn't want to plant flowers with me. She liked to help me water the plants after I finished planting them. After helping me water the succulents, she then asked, "Can I plant a flower?" Children have the tendency to change their minds about doing an activity after they have seen someone else do it. Just like in this situation, she didn't want to plant flowers in the beginning, but after, decided she wanted to try. She is 3 and a half years old and she can ask me what she wants to do. That means she has good language skills. She said she was able to shovel and do it by herself. That means she can express her idea. She followed the process of planting the flower with me. She remembered to plant the succulent in the pot, and then put the rocks on the top of the dirt. She was capable of imitation and has a good memory.

種植 Planting

Las Americas EES Joanne Yu
7/12/2020

瞳瞳用鏟子鏟一些泥土放到花盆裡.
(20年7月12日)

Ellie is shoveling dirt into the flowerpot.
(July 12th, 2020)

瞳瞳把肉質植物種在盆內.

Ellie is planting the succulent in the pot.

瞳瞳把裝飾石頭放在花盆內.

Ellie is placing the decorative rocks in the flowerpot.

瞳瞳澆刚種好的植物.

Ellie is watering the plant after planting and decorating.

背景：

自從20年3月17日起，因新冠肺炎疫情，我必须宅家，我花額外的時間在後花園裡.我的侄女瞳瞳Ellie現在3歲半,多數講中文.她喜歡戶外活動和玩水.於是她常常跟著我.這個"學習故事"是這樣開始的.

Background

Due to COVID-19, shelter in place has been effective since March 17, 2020. I have been spending this extra time at home, working in our backyard. My niece Ellie is three and a half years old and speaks mostly Chinese. She enjoys being outside and playing with water, so she often accompanies me. This is the start to my " learning story".

發生的事情：

瞳瞳,今天早上當你看見我種花後，你說你也想種，於是你拿起鏟子鏟起泥土，放在花盆内.你說你自己能做，不用我帮，我說: "很好，証明你很独立." 然後，你問我: "這花花放在哪裡?".我教你怎樣放入泥内，你把花種入泥内後，然後用裝飾石頭压住泥土，最後，用花洒澆水.

What Happened?

You saw me planting flowers and wanted to try it this morning, so you shoveled the dirt into the flowerpot. You said you were able to do it with no help. I said, "That's good, you're very independent." And then you asked me, "Where does the flower go?" I taught you how to plant the flower within the dirt. After you put the flower into the dirt, and then you placed decorative rocks on the top, finally you watered it.

Figure 4.4 Original Learning Story "Ellie Planting a Flower," by Joanne Yu

這意味着什麼：

在後花园，瞳瞳開始只想玩水，不想跟我種花，當我種完花後，叫她浇水，她很樂意，浇完水後, 瞳瞳問我："我可不可以種花花？"小孩子有時是這樣，當有機會看到你做的東西後，覺得有興趣，就有可能改變主意，想做她原來不想做的東西.她只有三歲半，能運用整句句子來問，說明她有好的語言能力. 她說她自己能用鏟子鏟泥，不用我幫，她把泥裝在盆內，這說明她有表達自己想法的能力.然後她學我那樣，將植物種入盆內，把小石頭壓住泥土.這說明她有模仿能力.

What Does This Mean?

When we first started going out into the backyard, she only wanted to play with water. She didn't want to plant flowers with me. She liked to help me water the plants after I finished planting them. After helping me water the succulents, she then asked, "Can I plant a flower?" Children have the tendency to change their minds about doing an activity after they have seen someone else do it. Just like in this situation, she didn't want to plant flowers in the beginning, but after, decided she wanted to try. She is 3 and a half years old and she can ask me what she wants to do. That means she has good language skills. She said she was able to shovel and do it by herself. That means she can express her idea. She followed the process of planting the flower with me. She remembered to plant the succulent in the pot, and then put the rocks on the top of the dirt. She was capable of imitation and has a good memory.

下一步計劃：

1. 學詞語：泥土，肉質植物，種
2. 數學：學數1至10
3. 培養種花興趣
4. 植物需要水

Next Steps:

1. Learn Vocabulary: dirt, succulent, plant
2. Learn to Count from 1 to 10
3. Gardening as a Hobby
4. Plants Need Water to Survive

家長看法：

我告訴瞳瞳的爸爸媽媽，瞳瞳今天種花，并澆水。她爸爸很高興，熱愛花草樹木，是好事，他說洗米水很好，以後會叫瞳瞳一起去後院用洗米水澆檸檬樹，花和她種的肉質植物.

Parent's Comment

I told Ellie's parents that Ellie planted and watered a succulent today. Her dad was happy to know Ellie was engaging with nature. Her dad said rice water is good for plants, he will bring her with him to water the lemon tree, flowers, and the succulent that she planted in the backyard.

The closing section of the Learning Story included a response from Ellie's father, who noted the cultural and familial practice of using rice water to water plants.

> **家長看法：** 我告訴瞳瞳的爸爸媽媽，瞳瞳今天種花，并澆水。她爸爸很高興，熱愛花草樹木，是好事，他說洗米水很好，以後會叫瞳瞳一起去後院用洗米水澆檸檬樹，花和她種的肉質植物.
>
> **Parent's Comment:** I told Ellie's parents that Ellie planted and watered a succulent today. Her dad was happy to know Ellie was engaging with nature. Her dad said rice water is good for plants, he will bring her with him to water the lemon tree, flowers, and the succulent that she planted in the backyard.

More Story Insights

In addition to all the precise observations and comments that Joanne included in the Learning Story, you also see Ellie's understanding of the sequence of planting and caring for the plants. She knows what to do first, second, and last. She is independent in her actions, reflecting a solid schema for this particular sequence of events. Sequencing events is a common acquisition in the preschool years. It is interesting that Joanne noted that at first Ellie was reluctant to help. It is as if she needs to watch and understand the sequence before she will act herself.

Sahara's Learning Story for Alexandra: "Alexandra Reading Aloud"

Sahara presented her Learning Story about 4-year-old Alexandra's book "reading" at a mid-October meeting of the Las Americas inquiry group (Figure 4.5).

Sahara wrote the story first in Spanish and then translated it into English for the inquiry group. The story chronicles Alexandra "reading" several books aloud in the book area. Sahara selected six photographs that she took of Alexandra's reading to feature in the Learning Story, and she also presented a video snippet of Alexandra reading. Sahara grouped the six photographs in three pairs, and each pair shows two slightly different actions, indicating the range of Alexandra's reading actions. Sahara noted that Alexandra held the books with her left hand and turned the pages with her right hand, and that Alexandra role played the way adults read books.

In the first section of the Learning Story, Sahara narrated her own internal process as a teacher inquirer documenting Alexandra's language and literacy learning.

> **What is the History? What Happened?**
>
> Alexandra, this afternoon I saw you reading in the book area. You were sitting on the small sofa, holding a book in your hands. I realized that you were "reading" out loud.
>
> I watched you move your lips, but I could not hear what you were saying because the other children were talking around you. I found it very interesting to see how you read, and I was curious to hear your reading. Then I decided to take a video and then listen to what you said. I understood that you were "reading" the story, you looked at the drawings, and I think you were describing the images in the book. Despite the noise you did not get distracted, you continued to focus on your book. You held the book with your left hand while turning the page with your right hand.

Alexandra Reading Aloud

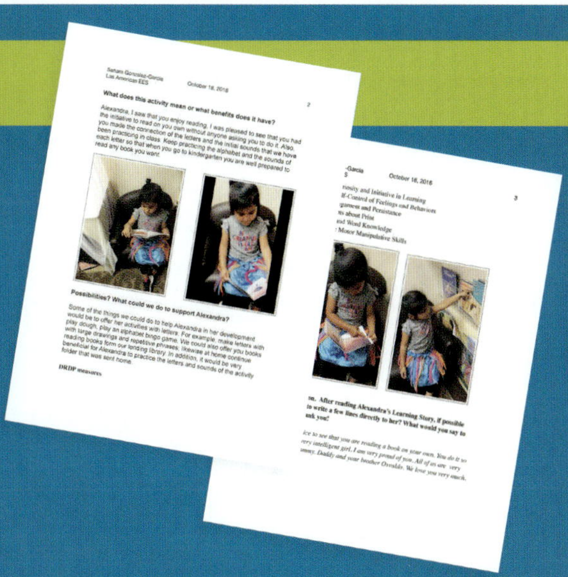

Sahara Gonzalez-Garcia,

Las Americas EES

October 18, 2018

What Is the History? What Happened?

Alexandra, this afternoon I saw you reading in the book area. You were sitting on the small sofa, holding a book in your hands. I realized that you were "reading" out loud.

I watched you move your lips, but I could not hear what you were saying because the other children were talking around you. I found it very interesting to see how you read and I was curious to hear your reading. Then I decided to take a video and then listen to what you said. I understood that you were "reading" the story, you looked at the drawings and I think you were describing the images in the book. Despite the noise you did not get distracted, you continued to focus on your book. You held the book with your left hand while turning the page with your right hand.

I could hear you said the word *pez* (fish) and *queso* (cheese). You paused for a moment. It seemed as if you had remembered the initial sound of the letter "P" and "Q". You put your lips together as if to emphasize the initial sound of those letters. Sometimes, you would point to the drawings or words with your finger. Your friends came close to you, but you continued reading your book. After you finished reading you returned the book to its place on the bookshelf.

What Does This Activity Mean or What Benefits Does It Have?

Alexandra, I saw that you enjoy reading, I was pleased to see that you had the initiative to read on you own without anyone asking you to do it. Also, you made the connection of the letters and the initial sounds that we have been practicing in class. Keep practicing the alphabet and the sounds of each letter so that when you go to kindergarten you are well prepared to read any book you want.

Possibilities? What Could We Do to Support Alexandra?

Some of the things we could do to help Alexandra in her development would be to offer her activities with letters. For example, make letters with play dough, play an alphabet bingo game. We could also offer you books with large drawings and repetitive phrases; likewise, at home continue reading books form our lending library. In addition, it would be very beneficial for Alexandra to practice the letters and sounds of the activity folder that was sent home.

DRDP Measures

1. ALT-REG 4: Curiosity and Initiative in Learning
2. ALT-REG 5: Self-Control of Feelings and Behaviors
3. ALT-REG 6: Engagement and Persistence
4. LLD 7: Concepts about Print
5. LLD 9: Letter and Word Knowledge
6. PD-HLTH: Fine motor manipulative Skills

Parents' Opinion

After reading Alexandra's Learning Story, if possible, would you like to write a few lines directly to her? What would you say to Alexandra? Thank you!

Daughter, how nice to see that you are reading a book on your own. You do it so well. You are a very intelligent girl. I am very proud of you. All of us are very proud of you, mommy, Daddy, and your brother Osvaldo. We love you very much.

Hija, que linda tu solita leyendo un libro, que bien lo ases, eres una niña muy inteligente. Estoy muy orgullosa de ti, Estamos muy orgullosos de ti; Mami, Papi y tu hermano Osvaldo.
"Te queremos mucho"

Figure 4.5 Original Learning Story "Alexandra Reading Aloud," by Sahara Gonzalez-Garcia

I could hear that you said the word *pez* (fish) and *queso* (cheese). You paused for a moment. It seemed as if you had remembered the initial sound of the letter "P" and "Q." You put your lips together as if to emphasize the initial sound of those letters. Sometimes, you would point to the drawings or words with your finger. Your friends came close to you, but you continued reading your book. After you finished reading you returned the book to its place on the bookshelf.

Sahara also chronicled and described the playful aspects of Alexandra's book reading, her playing with sounds—"I could hear that you said the word *pez* (fish) and *queso* (cheese). You paused for a moment. It seemed as if you had remembered the initial sound of the letter 'P' and 'Q'"—as well as Alexandra's intense concentration as she continued reading her book even when her "friends came close" to her.

In the next section, Sahara gave Alexandra more encouragement to continue reading and practicing:

What Does This Activity Mean or What Benefits Does It Have?

Alexandra, I saw that you enjoy reading. I was pleased to see that you had the initiative to read on your own without anyone asking you to do it. Also, you made the connection of the letters and the initial sounds that we have been practicing in class. Keep practicing the alphabet and the sounds of each letter so that when you go to kindergarten you are well prepared to read any book you want.

In the "Possibilities" section, Sahara offered next steps to support Alexandra's interest in reading, such as playing with play dough to make letters (play with manipulatives) and playing an alphabet bingo game (rule-governed play). Sahara also noted the DRDP measures that the Learning Story documents.

Possibilities? What Could We Do to Support Alexandra?

Some of the things we could do to help Alexandra in her development would be to offer her activities with letters. For example, make letters with play dough, play an alphabet bingo game. We could also offer you books with large drawings and repetitive phrases; likewise, at home continue reading books from our lending library. In addition, it would be very beneficial for Alexandra to practice the letters and sounds of the activity folder that was sent home.

DRDP Measures

ALT-REG 4: Curiosity and Initiative in Learning

ALT-REG 5: Self-Control of Feelings and Behaviors

ALT-REG 6: Engagement and Persistence

LLD 7: Concepts about Print

LLD 9: Letter and Word Knowledge

PD-HLTH: Fine Motor Manipulative Skills

In the Family Response section, Alexandra's mother, Maciel, writes a note (originally in Spanish) admiring Alexandra's reading and how the whole family is proud of her.

Daughter, how sweet it is that you are reading a book on your own, you do it so well, you are a very smart girl. I'm very proud of you. We are very proud of you. Mommy, Daddy and your brother Osvaldo. We love you so much.

One month later in November, during the next meeting of the inquiry group, Sahara followed up with the group about steps that were suggested in the group's October meeting. Sahara spoke with Alexandra about books at home and discovered that Alexandra only had one book at home. Sahara also shared the video of Alexandra reading the book in the classroom with Maciel, who said that she is not able to read books with her daughter at home. Sahara told Maciel that Alexandra also likes to write in her journal at school and to do the letters in the home-school packet. Sahara suggested that they visit the local public library, and she gave Maciel small blank cards so Alexandra could practice writing the letters at home. She suggested that Alexandra start with four letters at a time, capital and lower-case letters together, and then they can play a Go Fish game. Maciel said that sounded like a good idea as Alexandra likes to copy letters at home.

More Story Insights

In this Learning Story you see the combination of literacy learning with play. Alexandra is reading. Her behaviors are typical early reading behaviors where children playact a real observed behavior that they aspire to. She is trying on what it means to be a reader. She includes many aspects of reading, including turning the pages as she reads, focusing on the print as well as the pictures, and making connections between letter sounds and letter representations. All of this is in the context of play and a playful situation.

Daniel Meier's Learning Story for Lily: "Little Star is Sleeping"

I (author Daniel) have been volunteering one morning a week in a preschool classroom in a public school district, conducting whole class and small group read-alouds of books about nature and the outdoors, and the children created watercolor paintings and dictation based on the books. I wrote "Little Star is Sleeping" (Figure 4.6) after working with 4-year-old Lily, who was always quite attentive and engaged during the read-alouds and the painting and dictation. Lily was enthralled with Grace Lin's *A Big Mooncake for Little Star*.

Lily extended her dictation and watercolor painting in playful ways, adding more and more dictation on the small cards that I used for writing down the children's dictation. Lily wanted to tape together the three large pieces of paper on which she had used watercolors, and then taped the small cards with her dictation on the large paper.

At the beginning of the Learning Story, I noted Lily's playful approach to engaging with the book and its story.

> **What Happened? What's the Story?**
>
> Dear Lily,
>
> Last week, I read Grace Lin's *A Big Mooncake for Little Star* to the whole class. As I read the book, you looked as if you were really enjoying the story, listening to what would happen to the moon and to Little Star, and looking at the bold black and golden-yellow illustrations, beautifully created by Grace Lin. You also enjoyed acting out small gestures of eating the mooncake, nibble by nibble, just as Little Star did in the story, and at the end of the story, when I asked where the mooncake went, you said in Little Star's tummy. You certainly tracked and followed the whole story well.

"Little Star Is Sleeping"— A Learning Story About Lily's Drawing and Dictation

Daniel Meier

22 January 2020

What Happened? What's the Story?

Dear Lily, Last week, I read Grace Lin's *A Big Mooncake for Little Star* to the whole class. As I read the book, you looked as if you were really enjoying the story, listening to what would happen to the moon and to Little Star, and looking at the bold black and golden-yellow illustrations, beautifully created by Grace Lin. You also enjoyed acting out small gestures of eating the mooncake, nibble by nibble, just as Little Star did in the story, and at the end of the story, when I asked where the mooncake went, you said in Little Star's tummy. You certainly tracked and followed the whole story well.

Then, after I read the story with the whole class on the rug, you sat at a table with three other children to use the watercolor paints and to do dictation about your drawing. I wasn't sure you wanted to paint and dictate something about *A Big Mooncake for Little Star*, but I went ahead and opened up the book and propped it open on the table for you and your friends to look at, and possibly to get inspiration and ideas from for your painting and even dictation. You first started by carefully painting small splotches of paint on your paper. You worked slowly and with care, dipping your brush into the cup of water, and then brushing off extra water and then selecting a color, which you carefully applied to the paper. You were careful not to mix the colors, and when I asked you to help a younger child next to you, you did; you showed that child how not to mix the paints on the color palette, and instead to wipe the water and color off before selecting a new color.

When you were done painting and it was time for your dictation, you easily and eagerly dictated about the story, without even looking back over the book's words or pictures either on your own or with me. You watched as I wrote down your dictation on five separate, small pieces of paper; when you were done, I showed you how to fold the tape so that the pieces of paper would adhere to the paper. You then placed the tape on the back of each piece of paper, and then pressed it down on the paper in the correct order of your dictation, along with a bit of my help with the reading back of the dictation. You then wanted to tape your watercolor painting to your dictation by placing tape in the middle to make one large, combined painting and drawing.

What Is the Significance of the Story?

You showed how much you loved *A Big Mooncake for Little Star* and also how much you loved listening to the story, could follow the storyline and the plot, and how engaged you were in your watercolor painting and in your dictation. You also enjoyed learning how to tape the pieces of dictation to the paper, and to organize them in the correct sequence. This really shows to me how deeply you love stories and books, and how much care and thought you put into your own connections to stories and books, and in this case a beautiful story of a mooncake and the love between a mother and her child. I also learned how much knowledge you have about early literacy, and the function of print and words and pictures to tell a story and to have meaning.

What New Ideas Arise from This Story?

I am wondering how we might explore these new directions as you listen to more books and do more painting and dictation:

1. Share your painting and dictation with the whole class
2. Try to "read" back your dictation
3. Help the younger children with their painting and dictation
4. Practice copying and writing some words from the books
5. Practice writing some sounds for your dictation

Family Response (forthcoming)

Figure 4.6 Original Learning Story "Little Star Is Sleeping: A Learning Story About Lily's Drawing and Dictation," by Daniel Meier

Lily's playful acting out of Little Star's actions during the read-aloud of the book set the stage for Lily's playful watercolor painting, dictation, and taping of the papers to make a larger product.

I narrated this set of connections in the "What Happened?" section:

> When you were done painting and it was time for your dictation, you easily and eagerly dictated about the story, without even looking back over the book's words or pictures either on your own or with me. You watched as I wrote down your dictation on five separate, small pieces of paper; when you were done, I showed you how to fold the tape so that the pieces of paper would adhere to the paper. You then placed the tape on the back of each piece of paper, and then pressed it down on the paper in the correct order of your dictation, along with a bit of my help with the reading back of the dictation. You then wanted to tape your watercolor painting to your dictation by placing tape in the middle to make one large, combined painting and drawing.

Lily took the initiative to expand the activity to create a larger, more expansive product. I noted in the "What is the Significance of the Story?" section how much this Learning Story reveals Lily's early literacy knowledge about concepts of print, and how she explores early literacy and art through playfulness, creativity, and co-construction.

All of these examples illustrate how Learning Stories document children's developmental changes and deepen your understanding of children's social-emotional, physical, and linguistic growth. The Learning Stories also serve as a window into a particular child's specific construction of social relations, literacy knowledge, and cognitive schema.

Chapter Summary

This chapter highlighted how Learning Stories can focus on children's social-emotional, play, and language development, and how the presentation of these stories in inquiry groups provides educators with portraits of how individual children learn in these areas. Each Learning Story discussed shows how an individual child grapples with some aspect of their development with regard to self-regulation, independence, social relationships, languages, and academic learning. The inquiry group discussions around these stories provide teachers with additional insights and lenses with which to understand the learning of the children in their care, and provide the children's families with new information about their children's development in school.

Key Points

- The creation and sharing of Learning Stories about social interaction, play, and language also encourages inquiry group members to take on the perspectives of the children featured in a Learning Story.
- Ongoing inquiry group meetings allow educators to deepen and broaden their understanding of children's play, socialization, and language learning over weeks, months, and even years.
- The powerful emotions often shown in Learning Stories about children's efforts to make friends or to find the best words to initiate play make for stories that touch everyone, and in this communal process of the inquiry group these Learning Stories become "owned" by the group.
- When multiple Learning Stories are presented in an inquiry group session, and as the collection of Learning Stories accumulates over the course of months and years, group members are afforded a valuable professional opportunity to reflect on the varied developmental trajectories of individual children and to see how children's learning changes over time.

References

Curtis, D., & N. Jaboneta. 2019. *Children's Lively Minds: Schema Theory Made Visible*. St. Paul, MN: Redleaf Press.

DeVries, R., & B. Zan. 1994. *Moral Classrooms, Moral Children: Creating a Constructivist Atmosphere in Early Education*. New York: Teachers College Press.

DeVries, R., B. Zan, C. Hildebrandt, R. Edmiaston, & C. Sales. 2002. *Developing Constructivist Early Childhood Curriculum: Practical Principles and Activities*. New York: Teachers College Press.

Forman, G., & B. Fyfe. 2012. "Negotiated Learning Through Design, Documentation, and Discourse." In *The Hundred Languages of Children: The Reggio Emilia Experience in Transformation*, eds. C. Edwards, L. Gandini, & G. Forman, 3rd ed., 225–232. Santa Barbara, CA: Praeger.

Fosnot, C.T, & R.S. Perry. 2005. "Constructivism: A Psychological Theory of Learning." In *Constructivism: Theory, Perspectives and Practices*, ed. C.T. Fosnot. 8–38. New York: Teachers College Press.

Kroll, L.R. 2017. "Early Childhood Curriculum Development: The Role of Play in Building Self-Regulatory Capacity in Young Children." *Early Child Development and Care* 187 (5-6): 854–868.

Kroll, L.R. 2018. "How Documentation of Practice Contributes to Construction and Reconstruction of an Understanding of Learning and Teacher." In *Constructivist Education in an Age of Accountability*, ed. D.W. Kritt, 301–316. Cham, Switzerland: Palgrave MacMillan.

Maturana, H.R. & F.J. Varela. 1992. *The Tree of Knowledge: The Biological Roots of Human Understanding*, trans. R. Paolucci, Rev. ed. Boston: Shambhala.

Piaget, J. & B. Inhelder. 2000. *The Psychology of the Child*. New York: Basic Books.

Quinn, B. 2017. The Roots of Learning: Inquiry as a Form of Resistance at a Spanish Immersion Preschool. In *Documentation and Inquiry in the Early Childhood Classroom: Research Stories from Urban Centers and Schools*, eds. L.R. Kroll & D.R. Meier, 41–57. New York: Routledge.

Vygotsky, L.S. 1978. *Mind in Society: The Development of Higher Psychological Processes*. Cambridge, MA: Harvard University Press.

5 Integrating Inquiry and Learning Stories for Equitable Learning Opportunities

Across all roles and settings, advancing equity requires a dedication to self-reflection, a willingness to respectfully listen to others' perspectives without interruption or defensiveness, and a commitment to continuous learning to improve practice.

— NAEYC (2019, 5)

Opening Reflections

- How do inquiry groups help teachers create equitable learning environments and outcomes for young children and families?
- In what ways can Learning Stories help teachers develop strategies to support social, linguistic, and familial diversity and inclusivity?
- How do Learning Stories align with the principles and strategies from NAEYC's "Advancing Equity in Early Childhood Education" position statement?

Learning Stories provide the opportunity for teachers to receive feedback and insight about children's learning from different viewpoints for a deeper understanding of children's learning from multiple contributors. Children, coteachers, supervisors, coaches, parents, extended family, and the surrounding community may all have differing perspectives, contributing to a rich discourse and joint reflection. A community of learners is formed when committed educators come together to share, discuss, reflect, ponder, and question pedagogy and practice.

A deep and lasting commitment to professional growth needs to be at the heart of all teachers. NAEYC's "Advancing Equity in Early Childhood Education" position statement (2019) calls to action educators' commitment to advance equity through pedagogy and practice inside and outside the classroom settings: "All early childhood educators have a professional obligation to advance equity. They can do this best when they are effectively supported by the early learning settings in which they work and when they and their wider communities embrace diversity and full inclusion as strengths, uphold fundamental principles of fairness and justice, and work to eliminate structural inequities that limit equitable learning opportunities" (1). Working together in a community of practice that supports inclusivity, equity, and diversity is critical and requires a commitment by all educators.

The Learning Stories approach offers a vehicle to celebrate and honor differences, as well as similarities. This innovative approach provides a framework for educators to connect to children and families' lived experiences. Learning Stories provide a space for brave, meaningful conversations and reflection about the importance of honoring race, class, culture, gender, sexual orientation, ability, home language, national origin, indigenous heritage, religion, and other identities. These conversations help educators to address systemic racism and can be used to make visible learning that occurs inside and outside the classroom.

Furthermore, Learning Stories inquiry groups allow educators to slow down and focus on the strengths of children's unique historical, cultural, and social identities, and learning in multiple contexts. Teachers gain understanding about learning that occurs outside of classroom settings through the lens of the family as the central force in each child's education. Reflecting on and discussing Learning Stories together with other committed educators, with open hearts and minds, can have a powerful impact and transform teachers' perceptions and understanding about the children in their care.

Above all, Learning Stories highlight and make visible the tightly woven relationships between teachers, children, parents, and families (Carr 2001; Carr & Lee 2012, 2019), and showcase these deep connections as a beautiful tapestry representing the cultures, values, beliefs, and perspectives of others. Though a Learning Story is often written about and focuses on the child's learning experience, the benefits are not solely for the child, as the voice of the storyteller, child, parents, and families all provide occasion for a deeper, authentic connection to one another. Also, through the practice of inquiry, the values of each contributor to the Learning Story are revealed in the responses written to the child. The responses provide a window of insight into the important relationships with the child. Beyond the surface of the story, the process of analysis that occurs in inquiry groups helps identify the deeper learning and connection to the storyteller's values as a co-learner, along with the child.

Learning Stories and Inquiry Groups at Work

Individual inquiry groups vary in their size, composition, structure, and other specifics. You will notice some such variations in the following examples of the Placer and Nevada Counties inquiry group and the Las Americas inquiry group, which respectively showcase a newly formed group and a group that has been working together for several years.

Starting the Placer and Nevada Counties Inquiry Group

KidZCommunity agency serves Early Head Start (EHS) and Head Start children and families in Northern California and has implemented Learning Stories since 2013. Before my current work as a university professor, I (author Annie White) worked for the organization for approximately 20 years and helped oversee the pilot use of Learning Stories. After participation in a New Zealand Inspire study abroad trip led by Margie Carter (an early childhood professional and well-known author of numerous professional early education books), visiting their early care and education centers, examining teacher documentation, listening to New Zealand educators share about their journey writing Learning Stories, and hearing Wendy Lee (Director of the Educational Leadership Project Ltd and coauthor of *Learning Stories: Constructing Learner Identity in the Early Years* and *Learning Stories in Practice*) present on the history of their national curriculum and origins of Learning Stories, I became emphatic that this innovative approach to assessment could be incorporated at KidZCommunity Agency, in California, and beyond.

As previously mentioned in Chapter 2, teachers in California (and throughout the United States) feel they are drowning in required assessment methods, which have become a daunting, time-consuming task that many teachers dread (White, 2015). Studying in New Zealand provided the courage to seek change and advocate for Learning Stories in the US context. I was able to work with several EHS centers and home visitation programs that were willing to pilot using Learning Stories in conjunction with a required assessment tool, the Desired Results Developmental Profile (DRDP). The Learning Stories were used as contextual evidence to support the DRDP child assessment ratings. The outcome of the pilot was overwhelmingly positive, and teachers and home visitors found Learning Stories created (a) connection, (b) partnership, (c) the building of relationships, and (d) the value of shared understanding (White, 2015). Since my transition from KidZCommunity in 2015, the use of Learning Stories in the EHS program has continued and thrived with the support of Executive Director Denyse Cardoza, Child Development Unit, and through the coaching of Lindsey Shafer, Head Start/EHS Professional Development Coach. Lindsey participated in the online Learning Stories facilitator inquiry group, offered to start a new inquiry group for any KidZCommunity staff who were interested, and thus started the Placer and Nevada Counties inquiry group.

The Placer and Nevada Counties inquiry group primarily consisted of teachers and site supervisors from KidZCommunity and was first facilitated by Lindsey. After facilitating the inquiry group for a year, with monthly support from the Learning Stories facilitator group meetings, it was decided to encourage participants in the group to grow in the role of leadership, as well. Thus, Stacey Lafayette, EHS Site Supervisor at KidZCommunity, joined as a co-facilitator after she participated in the previous year's inquiry group. Stacey is also an advocate of Learning Stories and a KidZCommunity staff member who has been working side by side with Lindsey on implementing Learning Stories in the agency's practice since the initial pilot. Together, they invited early childhood educators across Placer and Nevada Counties in Northern California to join a small group of colleagues interested in exploring Learning Stories and the role documentation plays in deepening relationships with children, families, and colleagues.

KEY IDEA

Here Is an Outline of the Structure of the Inquiry Group Meetings

- Welcomes, refreshments, sign in, get settled, etc.
- Open the meeting with asking for volunteers to share documentation or stories during the meeting, then determine how much time is needed for each person based on how many participants want to share.
- Documentation and story sharing
    - Each person who shares provides context, shares their story or documentation artifact, and then the group gives feedback or asks questions to the presenter. The Thinking Lens protocol tool (Curtis & Carter 2017), adapted in collaboration with Ann Pelo, is used to help guide the reflection and discussion. The facilitator asks the participants to use the tool to help frame their reflection, analysis, and questions.
- Transition to article discussion
    - The group participants read the article ahead of the meeting.
    - Guiding prompt for reflection: "What stood out to you that you think is particularly interesting or important for our work?"
    - Open discussion and reflection
- Final reflection
- "What other questions do we have about our practices that we want to dive deeper into?"
- Follow up on resources to send out, reminder of date for next time, and appreciation for participation in the inquiry group

The Placer and Nevada Counties inquiry group community members included four EHS teachers, two EHS site supervisors, a Head Start teacher, a licensed marriage and family therapist, two senior caregivers, and a professional development coach. This inquiry group's experience, knowledge, and practice with Learning Stories ranged from being brand new to the Learning Stories approach to seven years of practice and implementation of Learning Stories. The inquiry group met once a month for two hours in the evening.

During the first inquiry group meeting, they set intentions by creating an outline of the structure for future meetings goals for the year, agreements, and discussed aspects of Learning Stories they wanted to explore and what questions they had about their practice (see chapter 1 on how to set up and facilitate Learning Stories inquiry groups).

The inquiry group implemented a consistent but flexible structure for each meeting that had two goals: sharing Learning Stories and Learning Stories article analysis through discussions on the readings. At each meeting, they began with story sharing and provided feedback and reflection to each other. Story sharing ranged from photo and oral stories to completed Learning Stories, with any and all forms of documentation being welcomed and encouraged. This Learning Stories inquiry group used the Thinking Lens for Reflection and Inquiry protocol (Curtis & Carter, 2017) to help guide discussion and feedback for stories that were shared.

Example of the Inquiry Group's Work and the Journey of a Learning Story

A Learning Story is a journey that includes many participants and follows different paths. The journey doesn't end with the writing of the story. The writing of the story is just the beginning. As you will see in the following example from the Placer and Nevada Counties inquiry group, one Learning Story becomes multiple stories providing different perspectives that extend learning and reflection.

Kelly Writes a Learning Story and Shares It with Her Inquiry Group

At one of the Placer and Nevada Counties inquiry group meetings, Kelly Rowe, an EHS teacher, and Ginger Park, her site supervisor (who is responsible for day-to-day operations), presented some challenges their center was having with Jacob, an "active" 2.7-year-old boy they weren't quite sure how to support. It became apparent through collaborative inquiry reflection that the environment was not equitable and set up for children who needed more active play. Instead, the teachers were trying to control Jacob's behavior through redirection rather than honor his interest by providing active engagement with the environment and a daily routine that allowed for significant outside playtime. Jacob is also biracial, an important factor for Kelly and Ginger to reflect on in relation to how they were responding to Jacob's behavior.

Research shows teacher biases toward young Black and Brown boys are evident in disproportionate preschool expulsion rates (Cyphert 2014; Gilliam et al. 2016). NAEYC (2019) recommends everyone to "acknowledge and seek to understand structural inequities and their impact over time. Take action when outcomes vary significantly by social identities (e.g., lopsided achievement test scores, number and frequency of suspensions or expulsions that disproportionately target Black and Latino boys, or engagement with certain materials and activities by gender). Look deeper at how your expectations, practices, curriculum, and/or policies may contribute (perhaps unwittingly) to inequitable outcomes for children and take steps to change them" (6). It is critical for teachers to be aware of any pedagogy and practices that contribute to possible structural inequities, especially for young boys, such as Jacob, who is biracial and a very active, energetic child.

Inquiry groups can help group members avoid a deficit model of thinking about children's behaviors. A critical challenge experienced by inquiry groups is supporting children whose cultural backgrounds don't match the teachers of the group; the group needs to learn together how to support the children through Learning Stories. By reflecting together through an inquiry group, it helped teacher Kelly to understand how she was mislabeling Jacob, and instead to look at his competencies, his strengths, and his social, cultural, and play talents. The ability to critically self-reflect through honest inquiry is vital. Lisa Delpit argues, "It is important to remember that children are individuals and cannot be made to fit into any preconceived mold of how they are 'supposed' to act. The question is not to necessarily how to create the perfect, 'cultural matched' learning situation for each ethnic group, but rather how to recognize when there is a problem for a particular child and how to see its cause in the most broadly conceived fashion." Delpit (1995) continues, "When a significant difference exists between the students' culture and the school's culture, teachers can easily misread students' aptitudes, intent or abilities as a result of the difference in styles of language and interactional patterns" (176).

Kelly identified the reasons for the difficulties she was having with Jacob which were that she was trying to control his behavior, and that there was not enough outdoors time. She did not want to be an educator who always says, "No." She was very open to feedback and suggestions. She was also able to relate this challenge to her own personal lived experience and herself as a learner, the need for freedom to explore, as she stated in her Learning Story: "You and I have some things in common; we both love finding out what makes things tick and we love solving problems." After many questions, conversation, and reflection with the inquiry group, Kelly had a plan for recognizing and responding to some of Jacob's opportunities for growth.

Following the inquiry group meeting, Kelly went back to the infant and toddler center and began to implement her new plan. She documented her observations of Jacob through Learning Stories. In addition, Kelly wrote a heartfelt Learning Story to the parent (discussed in detail in Chapter 6), which deepened her relationship and connection to the family. The week following the inquiry group meeting, she wrote the Learning Story, "Solving Puzzles, Finding Answers" (Figure 5.1), and her commitment and action to create equitable learning environments was reflected in it: "I asked several smart teachers for help and advice. I wanted to find ways to channel that curiosity and energy instead of trying to squash it down. I want you to feel like a brilliant scientist, a daring explorer, an amazing athlete . . . I don't want you to feel like the kid who's always doing something wrong."

In Kelly's analysis in the What Learning is Happening section of her Learning Story, she offers her reflections on the significance of the learning that occurred. Kelly's Learning Story analysis is composed of two parts: (1) reflection on Jacob's learning, and (2) her analysis of her own learning. This approach of including herself in the analysis is an example of the tenth principle of Child Development and Learning in NAEYC's "Advancing Equity in Early Childhood Education" position statement (2019): "Reflective practice is required to achieve equitable learning opportunities. Self-awareness, humility, respect, and a willingness to learn are key to becoming a teacher who equitably and effectively supports all children and families" (13).

Highlighting the self-reflection in her Learning Story, Kelly wrote:

> What I learned: (Yes, grownups still have things to learn, even teachers. Especially teachers.) You and I have some things in common; we both love finding out what makes things tick and we love solving problems. This week I learned about something called play schemas. It's a big, fancy way of saying "If someone likes to do this thing then they'll probably also like doing these other things." It was like a magic trick for finding fun things for you to do, things you can enjoy and still keep yourself and your friends safe. I'm not done searching for great ideas to share with you. We're going to learn a lot and we're going to have fun doing it.

The process of inquiry group reflection supports the writing and analysis of the learning and provides opportunity for educators to reflect deeply about their pedagogy and practice, help problem solve, see the child's interests and strengths, and further support the child's learning and growth. It is a conduit that propels teachers forward, to strive for inclusive and equitable practices for all children. It provides a way for teachers to identify their biases or areas of needed growth, and with

Solving Puzzles, Finding Answers

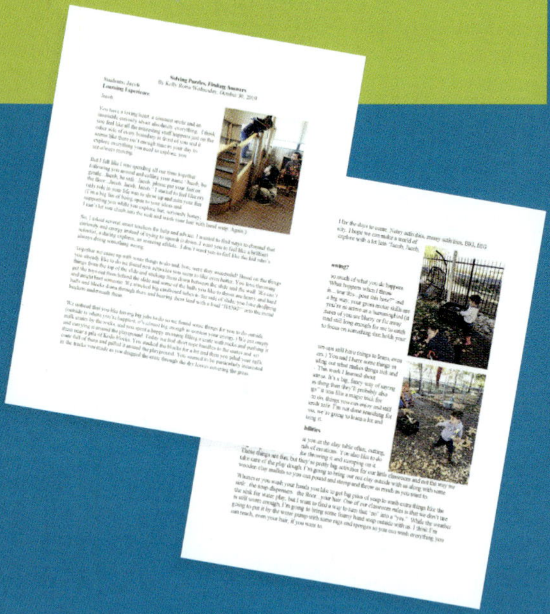

Kelly Rowe
Wednesday, October 30, 2019

Jacob,

You have a loving heart, a constant smile, and an insatiable curiosity about absolutely everything. I think you feel like all the interesting stuff happens just on the other side of every boundary in front of you and it seems like there isn't enough time in your day to explore everything you need to explore, you are *always* moving.

But I felt like I was spending all our time together following you around and calling your name "Jacob, be gentle . . . Jacob, be safe . . . Jacob, please put your feet on the floor . . . Jacob, Jacob, Jacob." I started to feel like my only role in your life was to show up and ruin your fun (I'm a big fan of being open to your ideas and supporting you while you explore, but, seriously honey, I can't let you climb into the sink and wash your hair with hand soap. Again.)

So, I asked several smart teachers for help and advice. I wanted to find ways to channel that curiosity and energy instead of trying to squash it down. I want you to feel like a brilliant scientist, a daring explorer, an amazing athlete . . . I don't want you to feel like the kid who's always doing something wrong.

Together we came up with some things to do and, boy, were they successful! Based on the things you already like to do we found new activities you seem to like even better. You love throwing things from the top of the slide and sticking them down between the slide and the wall. We can't get the toys out from behind the slide and some of the balls you like to throw are heavy and hard and might hurt someone. We attached big cardboard tubes to the side of slide, you love dropping balls and blocks down through them and hearing them land with a loud "BANG!" into the metal buckets underneath them.

We noticed that you like having big jobs to do so we found some things for you to do outside (outside is where you're happiest, it's *almost* big enough to contain your energy.) We put empty milk crates by the rocks, and you spent a happy morning filling a crate with rocks and pushing it and carrying it around the playground. Today we tied short rope handles to the crates and set them near a pile of Kodo blocks. You stacked the blocks for a bit and then you piled your milk crate full of them and pulled it around the playground. You seemed to be particularly interested in the tracks you made as you dragged the crate through the dry leaves covering the grass.

I have more ideas planned for the days to come. Noisy activities, messy activities, BIG, BIG things to spark your curiosity. I hope we can make a world of opportunities to learn and explore with a lot less "Jacob, Jacob, Jacob"

What Learning Was Happening?

What you learned: Jacob, so much of what you do happens around cause and effect. "What happens when I throw this . . . squash this . . . push this . . . tear this . . . pour this here?" and you like to experiment in a big way, your gross motor skills are in constant use. Although you're as active as a hummingbird (it seems like most of my pictures of you are blurry or far away because you don't often stand still long enough for me to catch up with you) your ability to focus on something that holds your attention is impressive. What I learned: (Yes, grown-ups still

Figure 5.1 Kelly's Learning Story for Jacob

have things to learn, even teachers. Especially teachers.) You and I have some things in common, we both love finding out what makes things tick and we love solving problems. This week I learned about something called play schemas. It's a big, fancy way of saying "If someone likes to do this thing then they'll probably also like doing these other things." It was like a magic trick for finding fun things for you to do, things you can enjoy and still keep yourself and your friends safe. I'm not done searching for great ideas to share with you. We're going to learn a lot and we're going to have fun doing it.

Opportunities and Possibilities

What we can try next: I see you at the clay table often, cutting, rolling, and shaping all kinds of creations. You also like to do big things with the clay, like throwing it and stomping on it. Those things are fun, but they're pretty big activities for our little classroom and not the way we take care of the play dough. I'm going to bring our red clay outside with us along with some wooden clay mallets so you can pound and stomp and throw as much as you want to.

Whenever you wash your hands you like to get big piles of soap to wash extra things like the sink . . . the soap dispensers . . . the floor . . . your hair. One of our classroom rules is that we don't use the sink for water play, but I want to find a way to turn that "no" into a "yes." While the weather is still warm enough, I'm going to bring some foamy hand soap outside with us. I think I'm going to put it by the water pump with some rags and sponges so you can wash everything you can reach, even your hair, if you want to.

Figure 5.1 Kelly's Learning Story for Jacob

humility acknowledge they are learners too. Kelly demonstrated NAEYC's charge (stated below) to address one's own biases through self-reflection:

> **When early childhood educators use inclusive teaching approaches, they demonstrate that they respect diversity and value all children's strengths. Early childhood educators can model humility and a willingness to learn by being accountable for any negative impacts of their own biases on their interactions with children and their families. They can work to ensure that all children have equitable access to the learning environment, the materials, and the adult-child and child-child interactions that help children thrive. Early childhood educators can recognize and support each child's unique strengths, seeking through personal and collective reflection to avoid biases—explicit or implicit—that may affect their decision making related to children. (NAEYC 2019, 5)**

Continuing the Learning Story Journey: Lindsey's Story

After Kelly completed the Learning Story and presented it to her inquiry group, she emailed it to Lindsey, the EHS Professional Development Coach and inquiry group co-facilitator, and asked for feedback. Lindsey decided to respond to Kelly's Learning Story in the form of a Learning Story back to Kelly titled, "With Challenges Come Triumphs" (Figure 5.2). In this Learning Story, Lindsey identifies Kelly's humility as a life-long learner, adds reflection on the positive nature of her writing style, and includes "possibilities" or next steps to help Kelly continue her work with Jacob.

Lindsey Shares Her Story with Her Inquiry Group

Lindsey's reflections on Kelly's work with Jacob provided an opportunity for her to extend her own learning and build on her work with Kelly as a Professional Development Coach. She decided to share both her and Kelly's Learning Stories with her own Learning Stories facilitator inquiry group. The group offered additional questions for both Lindsey and Kelly to consider. Here is an example of some excerpts from

With Challenges Come Triumphs: A Response to Solving Puzzles, Finding Answers

Lindsay
11/12/19
Learning Experience

Kelly,

It means so much to me that you're reaching out—you should share and be happy with this story! I have SO much I want to share back with you about it. Thank you for your patience while I reflected and gathered my response. I wanted to honor you and give you the focused attention and presence that you and this story deserve.

First off, your title, "Solving Puzzles, Finding Answers" is immediately engaging and drew me right in to want to read more. Your writing style in general is incredibly engaging and has an intangible quality about it that I just adore. You found a way to talk about a challenging and trying time for not only you and Jacob, but for your whole school community and to express it in a way that is authentic, strength-based, and honest. Learning stories are a great way to write about challenges but finding the voice to tell those stories in can sometimes be tricky. I agree with your reflection and think you have found that voice here.

You are building a positive learner identity for Jacob right from the beginning when you mention his "loving heart, a constant smile, and insatiable curiosity about absolutely everything."

You have found a way to paint a picture with your words that captures Jacob and your experiences with him so genuinely and accurately, while maintaining a strength-based approach.

You take the reader on a journey with you over the past weeks by writing about your process. From what you were observing, to asking for advice, to implementing new strategies including the tubes, the crates, the blocks, and the ropes on the crates.

I especially appreciate your interpretation where you write about what he is learning, but expand to what you are learning, because, yes, teachers are always learning too! I found this approach to the interpretation (breaking into the two parts) incredibly refreshing, creative, exciting, and transformative.

~Lindsey

What Learning Was Happening?

As I read your story, my heart swelled with pride, excitement, joy, and deep gratitude; for you, for Jacob, and for this journey you are on together. I am in awe of the vulnerability you show as a teacher and human being in this story.

When I had left after our time together towards the end of October, I must admit I was worried I was too harsh. Then, I received this beautiful story, written about your challenges but also your triumphs as you work through your day to day together. I am deeply grateful for your ability to take and receive feedback, both constructive and positive, and implement strategies for him so quickly and effectively. I am also grateful for getting to reflect together in person about our feedback meeting and share our perspectives over the weeks as we checked in together.

Opportunities and Possibilities

Kelly, I am putting together a resource on "heavy work" activities to support you and Jacob in the classroom with new and various ideas you can both explore and get curious about together (see attached). I will also continue to share with you all my knowledge and resources on schemas in children's play and reflect with you on children's interests as they change and develop.

Figure 5.2 Lindsey's Story Written to Kelly

the Learning Stories facilitator inquiry group meeting minutes from when Lindsey presented Kelly's Learning Story and her own Learning Story response to Kelly:

- **Learning Stories Presentation by Lindsey, Placer and Nevada Counties (KidZCommunity) Inquiry Group** — Lindsey shared a Learning Story from a teacher (Kelly Rowe) "Solving Puzzles, Finding Answers," and also her response to the story as coach/ supervisor, "With Challenges Come Triumphs"
    - General reflection of both Learning Stories shared is that the teacher's goal was to revisit her relationships and interactions with a toddler and focus on the strengths of the child and her own growth to change classroom, materials, and activities to promote positive experiences based on her observations of the child's interests and learning dispositions/schemas. Lindsey's response centered on how teachers are learning, too, including her observations of the teachers' growth in context of her own growth as [an EHS] supervisor. Lindsey shared that this was the first time using the Learning Story format to write to adults.
    - General points from group discussion and reflection included:
        - How the interactions of Lindsey and teaching team were included in the response story.
        - How the story included personalized feedback to teachers, not universal "global feedback" as is common. Also, the idea of NZ Maori "Ako"—we are all teachers and learners"—was represented in the story as Lindsey wrote about herself and the teachers and child. A "parallel process" was reflected in the story with "Lindsey to Teacher" and "Teacher to Child."
        - The story was written with passion and included the use of "We" to narrate the story rather than "I" or "You" at times signifying that they are in it together. It is believed the stories can be used as evidence of professional growth of the teacher.
        - Questions posed to presenter: *What is involved in the relationship necessary to write a Learning Story to an adult/ teacher?* Some responses included: trust, risk, familiarity, comfort, confidence, authenticity, honesty, open to feedback, etc. When the writing "comes from your heart."

Based on the reflections and feedback given during the Learning Stories Inquiry Facilitator group meeting, Lindsey followed up and shared the questions posed by the group with Kelly, and an excerpt from their dialogue follows:

> **Lindsey:** The Learning Stories facilitator inquiry group was fascinated by your addition of "What I learned" to the interpretation section "What Learning Was Happening". They wanted to know what inspired you to add this piece to your Learning Story in addition to what Jacob learned.
>
> **Kelly:** As a child I always thought grownups had everything figured out; it was an intimidating goal [to grow up] "How am I ever going to get from here to there?" I believe that it's important to share with them [children] that we're always learning, that we [teachers] get confused, that we have feelings. I think we should share the learning process "I don't know that answer, let's find out together!" and, especially, to acknowledge when we've made mistakes and apologize when we're wrong.
>
> Also, as I am aware that Learning Stories are a way to share the nuances of play-based learning with parents, I am also tuned into the fact that parents will be reading this story and taking away their own impression. As a young mother I was quietly intimidated by my daughter's teacher, she seemed to know so much more about everything than I did. In sharing my continuing learning process, I hope that Jacob's mother sees that the two of us are a team, shoulder to shoulder, taking care of a kid we both love and learning as we go along.

Lindsey's final reflection: The initial question and challenge of how to support a child turned into a process of inquiry and collaboration that rippled far beyond the child, Jacob, and the teacher, Kelly. Kelly and Ginger have since written Learning Stories to Jacob's mom, Priscilla, honoring her important role and contributor as a parent.

Next Steps on the Journey

The journey of Kelly's Learning Story about Jacob started very simply. It began with Kelly's desire to understand more about her student, and how she could support him and learn more about who she is as a teacher. Other participants and voices joined this journey along the way including Ginger, the Placer and Nevada Counties inquiry group, Lindsey, her Learning Story facilitator inquiry group, and Jacob's mom. Inquiry doesn't stop; it evolves. With each voice added to a Learning Story, the opportunities for reflection and growth expand. Every inquiry group provides a way for the voices to be heard. The journey of Kelly's Learning Story continues in Chapter 6.

Las Americas Inquiry Group

As mentioned in earlier chapters, Las Americas Early Education School in San Francisco Unified School District has an on-site inquiry group that has been working together for several years. The group meetings have encouraged the teachers to explore more authentic forms of assessment that capture children's learning. This exploration led them to "discover" the power of Learning Stories to document and focus on children's strengths, skills, learning dispositions, and dreams. For example, while exploring the concept of families with immigrant children they realized the importance of exposing children to culturally relevant literature. Although the classroom library included books in Spanish and English, none of them spoke of the realities and complexities of migrant children and families who had to leave their countries of origin in search of a better future. Finding new books provided an opportunity to explore with children a potentially sensitive topic (immigration) from children's perspective and with a focus on their strengths, not on their needs.

The teachers decided to borrow books from the library about stories that resonated with the children's own life experiences about immigration. One of the books selected was in Spanish and English titled, *A Movie in My Pillow/Una Pelicula en mi Almohada,* by Jorge Argueta, a local author from El Salvador. The children enjoyed this collection of poems where the main character, young Jorgito, lives in the San Francisco's Mission District, a predominantly Latino community, but he hasn't forgotten his native El Salvador and writes and dreams of both the things he left behind, such as *pupusas*, a traditional Salvadoran dish of thick corn tortillas filled with beans or cheese, and the things he has learned in his new country.

In one poem he relates how he learned to speak English, but in his dreams he speaks in Nahuatl, the native language of his grandma's people, the Pipiles. The children and teachers learned that Pipiles are an indigenous people of El Salvador who speak Nahuatl, the language of the Aztecs. I (author Isauro) described that our school is also in the Mission District of San Francisco, where the author and the poem's main character lives. Just like Jorgito in Jorge Argueta's book of poems, many of the children in their classroom had "memories" from where their parents had emigrated. Argueta's poems served as a springboard to children's (and teachers') creativity and imagination. For example, based on Karen's memories of her family in Peru, the teachers were able to capture her knowledge, skills, learning dispositions, and dreams in a Learning Story titled, "Karen's Grandparents' Peru." Karen's and other children's stories were documented in Spanish and later translated into English.

A few children felt confident expressing their ideas in English, but the more complex their thinking, the more they chose to speak in Spanish, their home language. I shared this discovery in one of our inquiry group meetings as we reflected on how Karen talked in class about Peru, the country from which her grandparents emigrated many years ago. Karen often switched from Spanish to English when talking and at times she seemed more confident speaking in English. In one of those conversations in English with Karen the teachers learned that her grandparents now own and manage a Latin American souvenir shop in the city. Karen shared that her grandfather was on a plane on his way to Peru to visit their family, friends, and relatives. Karen said she longed to go to Peru because that is where she has many cousins and that she would love to meet and play with all of them. In a small group activity, Karen painted Peruvian-style houses and she said in Spanish, "The houses in Peru are colorful and have red brick roofs, also the houses are in the shape of a square and some have triangle tops."

As inquiring teachers (Meier & Henderson 2007; Meier & Stremmel 2010), educators often try to find meaning in the stories that children share. In conversations with Karen's grandma, I (author Isauro) found out that Karen had never been to Peru. In reflecting with other teachers on Karen's artwork and her dictation, we concluded that she shows curiosity about her identity and is intrigued by a far-away place she has gotten to know only from stories told by her grandparents. Karen visualizes the houses of her grandfather's country of origin and feels compelled to memorialize her interest in a painting, which is included below. We teachers at Las Americas believe it is our responsibility to actively seek to integrate family stories in the preschool curriculum.

In Karen's mind, the houses in Peru are painted in vivid colors with flowers all over, and that's what she decided to paint on a canvas with acrylic paints. In her imagination, Karen sees an airplane carrying her grandfather to Peru. An airplane became a prominent feature on her painting. Later on, Karen also requested we read in class a book about Peru. Our curriculum became greatly influenced by Karen's and other children's ideas of what they wanted to learn in class, and the teachers' role was to become partners in the multiple opportunities and possibilities to extend that learning. The following is a Learning Story I wrote to Karen (Figure. 5.3).

Isauro's Reflection

Working on this project to find books that reflect children's stories made us as teachers realize that we play a pivotal role in preserving the Spanish language in relation to family, culture, and traditions. If children lose their ability to speak Spanish in an effort to learn English, they risk losing a link to their own heritage (Edyburn, Quirk, & Oliva-Olson 2019; Magruder et al. 2013). In our classroom we have seen that second generation children (whose parents are immigrants and first generation) have more difficulty acquiring the basics of Spanish and feel much more comfortable speaking English in their social interactions with peers and siblings. Some children respond in English to bilingual parents, even though these parents address them in Spanish. The situation worsens in the case of grandparents who speak only Spanish, and children don't make the effort to communicate in Spanish, or do it in a very limited manner.

Reflections from Coteachers

What is the benefit of this class project for children?

The benefit of this project for the children is that they can learn something about their peers' families and also that there are different kinds of families. For example, there are children that have two houses because their parents are separated but this is still a family. Also, children can learn to accept and respect other children's experiences. — Teacher Sahara

The benefit for children in this project is that they can learn more about who their parents are. The children also learn to recognize differences that exist between this country and their parent's country of origin. Also, they learn about different foods and traditions and, more importantly, they learn that they have grandparents, aunts, uncles, and cousins in other places, other countries. Through this project they learned that they have an extended family even if they are not able to see them in person. — Teacher Alicia

What is the benefit for teachers?

The benefit for us teachers is that we learned where the families we serve come from and we have a better sense of the children's behaviors in relation to their family members. If we know more of the children's personal family stories, we can better understand them. We can cope better when difficult situations arise, and we can offer the right support when parents or children need it. — Teacher Sahara

The benefit for teachers is that we can help parents, in some way, integrate themselves into this country. By knowing families at a more personal level, we learned a little more of their journeys and we were in a better position to offer support with their children's learning. By knowing where they come from and what it took for them to get here, we broke barriers and assumptions and work together to help in their children's education, which might be different from the education they knew in their countries of origin. — Teacher Alicia

El Perú de los Abuelos que Karen Imagina

Sahara Gonzalez, Alicia Alvarez, y I.M. Escamilla
Mayo 2017

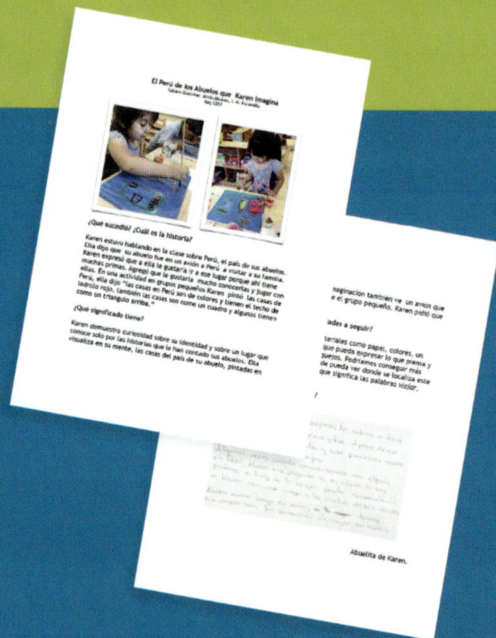

¿Qué Sucedió? ¿Cuál Es la Historia?

Karen estuvo hablando en la clase sobre Perú, el país de sus abuelos. Ella dijo que su abuelo fue en un avión a Perú a visitor a su familia. Karen expresó que a ella le gustaría ir a ese lugar porque ahí tiene muchas primas. Agregó que le gustaría mucho conocerlas y jugar con ellas. En una actividad en grupos pequeños. Karen pintó las casas de Perú, ella dijo "las casas en Perú son de colores y tienen el techo de ladrillo rojo, también las casas son como un cuadro y algunas tienen un triangulo arriba."

¿Qué Significado Tiene?

Karen demuestra curiosidad sobre su identidad y sobre un lugar que conoce solo por las historias que le han contado sus abuleos. Ella visualiza en su mente, las casas del país de su abuelo, pintadas en colores vivos con flores. En su imaginacíon también ve un avión que lleva a su abuelo a Perú. Durante el grupo pequeño, Karen pidió que leyéramos un libro sobre Perú.

¿Cuáles Son las Posibles Actividades a Seguir?

Podríamos ofrecerle a Karen materiales como papel, colores un lienzo y pinturas acrílicas para que pueda expresar lo que piensa y siente a través de dibujos y bosquejos. Podríamos consequir más libros sobre Perú y un mapa donde pueda ver donde se localiza este país. Podríamos hablar sobre lo que significa las palabras *viajar, tierra natal, y/o emigrar.*

¿Qué Opina la Familia de Karen?

Para nosotros es una sorpresa, los anhelos q' tiene Karen de conocer a sus primos y tios. A pesar de que Karen solo vio algunas fotos y sabe poco cosas acerca de nuestra ciudad de origen.
Algunas veces cuando conversamos con alguien en Perú, Karen nos pregunta si es alguna de sus primas o tios, a lo mejor pronto sorprendemos a Karen con una viaje a la ciudad de sus abuelos.
Karen nunca viajo en avion, talvez sus deseos son la sensación de viajar en avion.

Abuelita de Karen

Figure 5.3 Sahara, Alicia, and Isauro's Learning Story Written to Karen

As a whole, questions that emerged from working on this particular project are

- What is the best approach to support children's home language while learning English?
- What language do immigrant parents value most in the children's academic settings?
- What role do families play in preserving their home language?
- What role do stories and memoir play in early childhood education?

As we embarked on a new phase in our role as early childhood teachers of dual language learners (this was our second year as an officially designated Dual Language classroom), we realized that it is our responsibility to help children and parents see the value and beauty of Spanish. Spanish should be seen as a means through which we can reach academic achievement, enrich the children's school experiences, and support social emotional expression. NAEYC (2019) asks teachers to actively promote children's agency and specifically to "provide each child with opportunities for rich, engaging play and opportunities to make choices in planning and carrying out activities" (7). Learning Stories within the context of inquiry groups illustrate how to accomplish many of NAEYC's goals so that children explore who they are and value their "selves" from a very young age. The statement also advocates for treating all children fairly while honoring children as competent and capable of learning: "They [teachers] can create early learning environments that equitably distribute learning opportunities by helping all children experience responsive interactions that nurture their full range of social, emotional, cognitive, physical, and linguistic abilities; that reflect and model fundamental principles of fairness and justice . . ." (NAEYC 2019, 5).

Chapter Summary

In conclusion, we urge early childhood practitioners to incorporate NAEYC's statement (2019), "Advancing Equity in Early Childhood Education" as a call to action. We firmly believe that those who implement the Learning Stories approach (as demonstrated in the examples above), can meet the following charges to observe, document, and assess children's learning and development.

- Recognize the potential of your own culture and background affecting your judgment when observing, documenting, and assessing children's behavior, learning, or development.
- Approach a child's confusing or challenging behavior as an opportunity for inquiry. Consider whether these may be behaviors that work well for the child's own home or community context but differ or conflict with your family culture or the culture of your setting. How can you adapt your own expectations and learning environment to incorporate each child's cultural way of being?
- Also, consider the societal and structural perspectives: How might poverty, trauma, inequities, and other adverse conditions affect how children negotiate and respond to their world? How can you help each child build resilience?
- Use authentic assessments that seek to identify children's strengths and provide a well-rounded picture of development.
- For children whose first language is not English, conduct assessments in as many of the children's home languages as possible.
- If you are required to use an assessment tool that has not been established as reliable or valid for the characteristics of a given child, recognize the limitations of the findings and strive to make sure they are not used as a key factor in high-stakes decisions.
- Focus on strengths.
- Develop the skill to observe a child's environment from the child's perspective.
- Seek to change what you can about your own behaviors to support that child instead of expecting the child to change first.
- Recognize that it is often easier to focus on what a child isn't doing compared with peers than it is to see what that child can do in a given context (or could do with support).

It takes courage, dedication, and commitment for early care and education professionals to incorporate inclusive, equity-minded teaching practices, that reflect respect for diversity and value all children's strengths and abilities. Learning Stories offer teachers opportunity to zoom in and look closely at not only children's learning, but also at their own learning too. The Learning Stories approach provides an innovative pathway that honors the collective, diverse voices of teachers, children, parents, families, and community through the stories that capture the hearts and minds of all. Learning Stories inquiry groups provide time and space to reflect from the contributions of multiple perspectives. This process allows teachers to reflect on who they are, and what they value, while strengthening their identity as professionals.

As an educator of young children, you have been charged to act with integrity, honesty, and commitment. As stated in the recommendations listed above, you must begin with implementing observation, documentation, and assessment practices by looking rigorously inward to "recognize the potential of your own culture and background affecting your judgment when observing, documenting, and assessing children's behavior, learning, or development" (NAEYC 2019, 8). Teachers must actively promote children's agency and, specifically, "provide each child with opportunities for rich, engaging play and opportunities to make choices in planning and carrying out activities" (NAEYC 2019, 7). Diving deeper into Learning Stories within the context of inquiry groups illustrates how to accomplish many of the goals in the NAEYC equity statement so that children explore who they are and value their "selves" from a very young age, while teachers simultaneously continue their parallel journey as life-long learners.

Key Points

- Though a Learning Story is often written and focused on the child's learning experience, the voices of the storyteller, child, parents, and families all provide occasion for a deeper, authentic connection to one and another. Also, through the practice of inquiry, the values of each contributor to a Learning Story are revealed in the responses written to the child.
- The inquiry groups implement a consistent, but flexible structure for each meeting that has two goals: sharing stories and article analysis and discussions.
- A critical challenge experienced by inquiry groups is supporting children whose cultural backgrounds don't match the group; the group needs to learn together how to support each child through Learning Stories.

References

Argueta, J. 2001. *A Movie in My Pillow: Poems*. San Francisco: Children's Book Press.

Carr, M. 2001. *Assessment in Early Childhood Settings: Learning Stories*. Thousand Oaks, CA: Sage.

Carr, M., & W. Lee. 2012. *Learning Stories: Constructing Learner Identities in Early Education*. Thousand Oaks, CA: Sage.

Carr, M., & W. Lee. 2019. *Learning Stories in Practice*. Thousand Oaks, CA: Sage.

Curtis, D., & M. Carter. (2018). *Learning Together with Young Children: A Curriculum Framework for Reflective Teachers*, 2nd ed. St. Paul, MN: Redleaf Press.

Cyphert, A.B. 2014. "Addressing Racial Disparities in Preschool Suspension and Expulsion Rates." *Tennessee Law Review* 82 (4): 893.

Delpit, L. 1995. *Other People's Children: Cultural Conflict in the Classroom*. New York: New Press.

Edyburn, K.L., M. Quirk, & C. Oliva-Olson. 2019. "Supporting Spanish–English Bilingual Language Development Among Latinx Dual Language Learners in Early Learning Settings." *Contemporary School Psychology* 23 (1): 87–100.

Gilliam, W.S., A.N. Maupin, C.R. Reyes, M. Accavitti, & F. Shic. 2016. "Do Early Educators' Implicit Biases Regarding Sex and Race Relate to Behavior Expectations and Recommendations of Preschool Expulsions and Suspensions?" Research Study Brief. New Haven, CT: Yale University, Child Study Center.

Magruder, E.S., W.W. Hayslip, L.M. Espinosa, & C. Matera. 2013. "Many Languages, One Teacher: Supporting Language and Literacy Development for Preschool Dual Language Learners." *Young Children* 68 (1): 8–15.

Meier, D.R., & B. Henderson. 2007. *Learning from Young Children in the Classroom: The Art and Science of Teacher Research*. New York: Teachers College Press.

Meier, D.R., & A.J. Stremmel. 2010. "Reflection Through Narrative: The Power of Narrative Inquiry in Early Childhood Teacher Education." *Journal of Early Childhood Teacher Education* 31 (3): 249–257.

NAEYC. 2019. "Advancing Equity in Early Childhood Education." Position statement. Washington, DC: NAEYC. www.naeyc.org/resources/position-statements/equity.

White, A. 2015. "Creating New Pathways for Dialogue: Engaging Families in School Readiness." Dissertation. University of California, Davis.

Family Engagement and Learning Stories: Inclusion of Diverse Voices

6

In telling them [our stories], we are telling each other the human story. Stories that touch us in this place of common humanness awaken us and weave us together as a family once again.

— Rachel Naomi Remen (1996)

Opening Reflections

- How do Learning Stories strengthen relationships with families?
- In what ways can Learning stories be used to engage families in children's learning?
- What are Learning Stories strategies that can be used to include multiple voices and diverse perspectives?

Often diverse voices are excluded from child assessment practices. Child learning outcomes are based on teacher observations and frequently lack parent input. Parents are recipients of assessment reports rather than active partners and valued contributors (Curtis & Carter 2017). On occasion, teachers ask parents ways they might incorporate activities to support learning in the home setting. Yet, these parent contributions often take place after teachers complete assessments, and children's learning at home is not included in assessment ratings. Thus, a one-sided view of children's learning often dominates the results of child assessment outcome reports. However, including multiple perspectives in assessment practices that reflect children learning outside classroom environments is essential. Learning Stories offer an opportunity for collaboration of diverse voices reflecting together about young children's learning experiences, strengths, and dispositional learning, where children as learners engage in and relate to the learning process. Including multiple voices provides varying perspectives that reveal children's learning holistically in multiple settings. Including child, parent, and family member voices is central to Learning Stories and their use as an assessment approach (Carr & Lee 2019).

This chapter includes examples of family engagement through Learning Stories written to parents, by a guardian, by teachers at a California community college's early childhood department and laboratory school, and by teachers at a community college in Hawai'i who have been practicing writing Learning Stories for several years.

Learning Stories provide opportunity for teachers not only to learn about the children in their care, but also and equally importantly, to learn what families think and value about their children's learning. Learning Stories become a conduit or a framework for teachers to convey their deep care for children, while through reciprocity families are able to share with teachers their love, hopes, and dreams for their children. Beyond superficial relationships, Learning Stories help teachers create deeper connections and stronger relationships with parents and families (Hatherly 2006; Southcott 2015).

Teachers desire deep, meaningful relationships with families and seek innovative ways to connect with families. Yet, lack of time continues to be a barrier. Families are often overwhelmed with competing roles, trying to balance work, school, and home responsibilities. Teachers are feeling equally burdened with limited time due to increased work responsibilities, such as with time-consuming assessment methods. In spite of these challenges, teachers creatively find strategies to engage families in dialogue through the process of sharing Learning Stories. Teachers thoughtfully incorporate strategies to share Learning Stories and reflect together with families. Here are some sample strategies for how to engage families with Learning Stories:

- Use e-portfolios to send and elicit responses from parents in real time.
- Along with sending a Learning Story to a parent, send a note with a prompt question, such as, "Hi. I wanted to share the Learning Story I recently wrote about your child. I would love to know if you are seeing similar learning occurring at home, too."
- Read a "favorite" Learning Story to parents and child during regularly scheduled teacher-parent conferences.
- Incorporate time during parent meetings for parents to read their child's Learning Stories from the hard copy portfolio.
- Have children cook muffins as part of a lesson plan and offer at morning drop off to parents, set on a low table with the children's portfolios placed with a sign saying, "Welcome! Help yourself to the children's homemade muffins, grab your child's portfolio, and read the newest Learning Story with your child."
- Post sample Learning Stories in portable stands by sign-in area.
- Display Learning Stories in picture frames in high-traffic areas such as entry, hallways, or bathrooms.
- Share Learning Stories during morning meetings or small group time, in cozy areas, outside yards, or a reception area.
- Showcase a new Learning Story in a monthly family newsletter.
- Create a family area with a couch or other comfortable seating for children, families, and community members to read portfolio Learning Stories.
- Make hard copy portfolios available in the classroom for children and families to easily access.

Though this is not an exhaustive list of strategies, it offers some possible ways you can engage families with Learning Stories. Regardless of the method of engagement, it is essential that teachers who use e-portfolio or electronic methods to share Learning Stories carefully consider the importance of *also* including physical hard copy portfolios for young children to access. One should not replace the other. An e-portfolio is a great tool to engage and communicate with parents. A 2013 study on the use of e-portfolios in New Zealand revealed that parents felt better informed about their child's learning, and this led to increased confidence in approaching their children's teachers and talking with more interest about the Learning Stories (Higgins & Cherrington 2017). Hard copy portfolios need to be available for children to revisit, over and over again. The hard copy Learning Stories become a precious artifact that can be treasured by future generations.

The Building of Relationships

Writing Learning Stories is a powerful experience for the storyteller. In addition, sharing the stories and collaborating with parents can reshape and transform relationships. In Chapter 5 we shared the Learning Story written by teacher Kelly, "Solving Puzzles, Finding Answers." Kelly's story took a journey with many steps as the story was shared and expanded on by others. Here we discuss the next steps including how Kelly reached out to the parent of Jacob.

As discussed in Chapter 5, Lindsey, the Early Head Start (EHS) Professional Development Coach who is also the Learning Stories inquiry group facilitator, wrote a Learning Story in response to Kelly titled, "With Challenges Come Triumphs" and shared the story with her facilitator inquiry group. The members of this group decided to ask Kelly questions to dive deeper below the surface of the Learning Story.

This group asked Kelly about personal experiences related to the topic of her story. Note that each inquiry group should decide on their approach to asking more personal questions, but Lindsey decided because of the close, trusting relationship she had with Kelly, to email to her the following questions.

Facilitator Inquiry Group questions:

- Did Kelly's daughter have active experiences at her childcare program with a teacher who was "more knowledgeable"?
- How did Kelly's daughter's experience compare to Jacob's? Did she have exposure to active play or more "no" environments? Was she restricted?
- What did Kelly experience growing up?

In other words, were there any similarities between Jacob, Kelly, and Kelly's child in regards to being provided active play or more restrictive play environments?

To answer these questions, Kelly had to reflect on the story relative to her own personal experiences as a parent. Her responses revealed how, as she was an adventurous child, she related to Jacob's need for active play. She also discussed her own experience as a parent with a teacher who she felt was more knowledgeable.

Kelly's response: Before I became an early childhood teacher, my preschool experience revolved around my daughter, Molly, and her time at a city-run preschool. Molly received a heart transplant as an infant and didn't have contact with many other children in her early years because her suppressed immune system made her vulnerable to infection. As kindergarten approached, I wanted her to give her some socialization opportunities before she plunged into school. She was a quiet, serious, contemplative child. The teacher was focused on drawing her out and supporting her socialization. I was intimidated by the teacher, but she was kind and supportive and concerned about my well-being as well as Molly's. My feeling of inadequacy stemmed from my own feelings about my poverty, lack of education, and the fact that I was learning to parent a child with a medical condition, and although we had the finest medical care Stanford could provide, I had little family support and guidance for the everyday mothering. I was winging it like crazy and wondering if I was getting it right. I am passionate about EHS because if we had had access to a program like the one I'm in, the entire trajectory of our little family would have been altered.

As children, we rode our minibike and spent hours on the old-school metal playground nearby busily devising ways to use old parachute lines to lift each other up on to the fifteen-foot platform without using the stairs and rappelling down the side like Batman. Don't tell mom . . . . I wish I could say this freedom was reflected in my parenting, but I was a very conservative mother when it came to risks. I suspect it was the anxious backlash from having one child with a serious medical condition . . . . This is one of the many, many things I love about teaching, this never-ending circle of growth. They learn from me, I learn from them, we're all in it together.

Kelly's experience with the facilitator inquiry group gave her the idea to write a Learning Story directly to Jacob's parent, Priscilla, titled "Where Love Grows" (Figure 6.1). Kelly shared that at the time she wrote the Learning Story, the EHS program had just begun to write Learning Stories using an electronic platform, but did not yet have the option of sharing them electronically with families. Thus, Kelly printed hard copies of the Learning Stories and added them to the children's binder portfolios. In addition, Kelly often printed an extra copy of her "favorite" Learning Story to share with the families when they picked up their children at the center so they could take them home

Where Love Grows

By Kelly Rowe
November 25, 2019

Dear Priscilla,

We usually write Learning Stories for the children as we watch them doing wonderful things in the classroom, but I feel like, in a way, we are watching you in action in the classroom. When we see Jacob at his most tender, gently caring for his smaller classmates, smothering Harry in hugs, quietly tending to baby dolls, we're seeing him showing the kind of care he sees at home. When we see his sisters rush in to come pick him up at the end of the day and you and all the kids are so happy to be reunited after a busy day apart, we're seeing a warm family coming together.

Jacob came to school last week with a badly scraped up face; he had fallen while his sister was giving him a piggyback ride. We had to call you later to tell you that his injured nose was looking worse and he probably needed to have a doctor check it. You wanted to come immediately, but you had to wait until you could pick up the rest of your kids.

When you got to school you told Ginger [the site supervisor] and me that you were upset with his sister for dropping him. We both rushed to reassure you that her intentions were good and accidents happen, but I'm pretty sure you already knew that and you were just hurting for him and full of regret that you didn't anticipate the fall in order to protect him.

I don't think I'll ever forget when you looked at me and calmly confided, "I might rely on them too much, but I'm all we have."

"I'm all we have" you said. You didn't say, "I'm all alone" you didn't say, "I'm all they have" in that moment I felt the weight of your responsibilities and the depth of your love. I feel like you're the leader of a tight little tribe and you're all in this together.

My heart went out to you at our home visit the next week as you calmly described your earliest days without their dad. Caring for a newborn, trying to help Jacob deal with an absence he couldn't possibly understand, supporting your family as they mourned a profound loss in their young lives. And still, as you told the story, it didn't feel to me like you were even considering the impact on you, you were so focused on your kids.

Mothering is tough and no one can ever be certain of what the years ahead will bring. I know one thing, though, your children are deeply loved and, most importantly, they know it. That is a beautiful, strong foundation to stand on while they learn about their world.

I've been teaching for a long time. I've known a lot of parents, but I don't know if I've ever seen a mother as strong and focused and selfless as you. I'm so happy I've had a chance to watch you love your kids.

-Kelly

Figure 6.1 Learning Story Written to Parent

to read. However, Kelly decided on a different strategy to share the Learning Story with Priscilla. Instead of sending the Learning Story via email or handing over a hard copy, Kelly decided to *read* the Learning Story aloud to Priscilla. The experience was very emotional; Priscilla cried as Kelly read about Jacob.

The impact of the Learning Story written to the parent was a thread that strengthened not only the relationship among Jacob, his parent, Priscilla, and Kelly, but also with the site supervisor, Ginger Parks. A powerful message of respect, value, and deep care was evident in the Learning Story, which created an opportunity for an exchange of feelings for one and another. The depth of relationships continued to grow. Months later, as Ginger reflected on the story and had more time to get to know Priscilla, and Jacob, she wrote to Priscilla (Figure 6.2). This simple act strengthened the relationship that existed between the family and the staff at EHS.

The cords of these relationships cannot be easily broken. The strands are tightly woven through the deep care and love expressed in the voices and perspectives of caring teacher, coach, administrator, parent, and child. This is what family engagement and partnership is all about. The next section will showcase another model for promoting family engagement through Learning Stories in a collaborative community practice.

Ginger's Note to Priscilla, Jacob, and Joseph's Mom

Ginger, site supervisor
Tuesday, June 23, 2020

Dear Priscilla,

Over the past year, we have come to know you and your family. Your dedication to your family is apparent by how I have observed you with your children. You are calm and patient, understanding and flexible. When you are not around, I have witnessed your children being nurturing and empathetic towards others. This is a skill that young children learn by seeing others demonstrate when, where, how and why to practice them. It is very clear to me where they are learning these life tools.

During our conversation today, you mentioned that you wish you had us [the Early Head Start Program] in your life when you were 17. That your parenting skills would be "better". Well, although I appreciate your beautiful compliment, I want to acknowledge what you have accomplished before joining our Lincoln Early Head Start family. You have raised children that care for one another. They are curious children that feel safe to explore and experience life. Your children will not let the world tell them "no" as they have a determination that is powerful and limitless.

These family photos you have shared say it all! I want to thank you for sharing a peek into your family and I look forward to seeing more!

-Ginger

Figure 6.2 A Learning Story Follow-Up Note to a Parent

Collaborative Community of Practice: Ventura County Office of Education and University

> Teachers spoke about the relationships with the families and how Learning Stories led to a deeper connection with the children through sharing their written stories. — Lorena Ramos, Technical Assistance Specialist at Ventura County Office of Education

During the 2019–2020 school year, a diverse group of novice and veteran early childhood teachers (center-based teachers and family child care providers) convened at the Ventura County Office of Education to learn more about Learning Stories. This Learning Stories inquiry group was co-facilitated by me (author Annie White) and Lorena Ramos from the County Office of Education. Many of the participants were new to Learning Stories. The cohort began their journey with a thorough presentation on the Learning Stories elements. Like other groups in previous chapters of this book, this new Learning Stories inquiry group implemented a meeting structure and strategies for collecting and sharing documentation, and together they practiced writing Learning Stories.

The teachers met once a month, reviewing the components of Learning Stories, and gradually began writing Learning Stories to enhance their knowledge of the process. First, the inquiry group explored articles, sample Learning Stories, and participated in deep discussion on topics brought forth by the book, *Learning Stories in Practice,* by Margaret Carr and Wendy Lee (2019). An in-depth book study led to monthly chapter discussions and further reflection and analysis of each other's written Learning Stories. After months of laying a solid theoretical understanding of Learning Stories, the teachers began writing and sharing more and more of their own narrative stories and were given constructive feedback to hone their Learning Stories practice.

A common thread emerged from the narratives stories that the teachers wrote which focused on family engagement. Teachers spoke about how they built stronger relationships with parents and how Learning Stories led to deeper connections with children and families. During the monthly inquiry group meetings, there was discussion of possible strategies to engage families in contributing to teacher-written Learning Stories. Each month, participants shared about the strategies they used to elicit family responses. This led to further discussion and brainstorming additional ideas for family engagement. The ultimate goal was to increase parent and family voices, perspectives, and responses to Learning Stories.

Opportunities for Learning Stories Outside the Classroom

The work of engaging in the Learning Stories practice is not solely for teachers in the classroom but also for group facilitators, instructional coaches, administrators, and those involved in planning professional growth opportunities for their teaching community or staff. Learning Stories can be used as a framework, a philosophy towards assessment, and to reflect on both child and adult learning. We are all learners.

For those members of the early childhood education community who spend little or no time in the classroom, or even for those who do, family trips, cultural celebrations, holidays, field trips, special events, and so forth can provide opportunities to engage in the writing of Learning Stories. For example, I (author Annie White) have used annual summer trips to National Parks to write Learning Stories to my granddaughter, as I want to preserve the memory of these special times, and I hope that she will share these with our future family, too.

Annie's Personal Journey on Using Learning Stories at Home

I have been helping raise my granddaughter for the past nine years. Writing Learning Stories to her and sharing them with my granddaughter's parents has been a powerful way to convey my thinking about my granddaughter's learning. More importantly, I am able to share with my granddaughter my care, love, and awe of her as a competent, capable, resilient person. Below is a sample of a Learning Story I wrote and shared in our inquiry group (Figure 6.3).

Barefoot and Beyond

Annie White
October 23, 2019

Ariana, what a fabulous time we had together with Grandpa, Lorraine and Rod this summer. What an adventurous time we had visiting our beautiful National Parks: Yellowstone and Grand Tetons. Your fierce determination when faced with swarms of mosquitoes, hikes over mountains, hail, encounters with grizzly bears, and long drives along curvy roads amazed me. I was especially thrilled watching you bravely climb the tall tree. You looked up at the vast tree without any hesitation and set your mind to climb it. You were barefoot and determined. What a delight to watch you. You thoughtfully placed each foot, testing the strength of the branches. At times, you looked down at grandpa for reassurance but unwavering in your self-confidence. I have to admit, the higher you climbed, the more challenging it was for not only you but also for me too. I realized that part of being your grandma is to provide you opportunities that allow you to take risks so you can continue in your journey of learning. So, climb on Ariana, to the highest tree, mountains and beyond.

Much love, Grandma Annie

What It Means (What Learning Do I See Happening Here?)

Ariana, when you decided to climb the tall tree, you showed not only your bravery but, your ability to persevere when facing difficult tasks. Though it can be easy to give up when trying to accomplish challenges, your self-determination and confidence is evident by the way you approach difficulties. When you bravely climbed the tree, you showed your willingness to grow and work on mastering your climbing through practicing your balance, coordination, and inner strength. Carol Dweck refers to this as "Growth Mindset". This means that when you have a growth mindset, your abilities can be developed through dedication and hard work. This view creates a love of learning and a resilience that is essential for great accomplishments (Claro 2016). It is so wonderful to see your love for adventure, your willingness to take risks, and desire to try new challenges.

Opportunities and Possibilities (How Can We Stretch This Learning Further?)

Ariana, I hope to see you continue to climb not only trees (especially our pear trees in our orchard) but, I hope you will continue your love for heights and scale up and over rocks, to the highest mountain peaks, and beyond. Grandpa and I will continue to take you each summer to the National Parks for you to discover new trees, rocks, and mountains to climb. As we are reminded by *John Muir, "The mountains are Calling". So, listen carefully, as they are calling you to new adventures.

Ariana response 10/25/19 *"The higher I climbed, the easier it was because the branches were closer. I could see the mountains far away. My feet were sticky because of the sap. I would have climbed higher, but it was time to go."*

Ariana revisited 11/16/19 *"It was fun. It was fun because the higher I got, it was more challenging, and I like challenges."*

Family response *It is great to see you continue enjoying climbing and not being afraid to go high off the ground. It is a metaphor for all of life's accomplishments and challenges. It is important that you put forth effort and take initiative to try new things.* —Grandpa Jim

**Note- Ariana participated in a 3rd grade unit study on Yosemite National Park, which included the contributions of John Muir. Her class spent several days at Yosemite and the quote, "The mountains are Calling" was an important part of their study. However, the authors acknowledge the recent criticism of Muir and his views on Native Americans, yet felt that sharing the original Learning Story in its entirety is warranted.*

Figure 6.3 Original Learning Story "Barefoot and Beyond"

Family Voices

"Barefoot and Beyond" is also an example of a Learning Story written from the parent or guardian perspective rather than the teacher. Parent- and family-written Learning Stories are very powerful because they help teachers and children to learn more about the important relationships of the child and family. The Learning Story "Barefoot and Beyond" includes reflection by the child who revisited it. It is important to include the voices of children to make visible their own thinking as a learner. In addition, the storyteller can re-read or invite children (who are able to read) to read aloud their Learning Story, adding any additional child responses. Often, over time, Learning Stories show connection to previously written stories where threads of learning are interconnected, showing the children's developing dispositional learner identities. The practice of writing Learning Stories has helped strengthen my pedagogy as a university professor. Experiencing firsthand the impact it has had on my relationship with my granddaughter, the value of including multiple family members, and the importance of including the child voice has led me to focus more in my college courses on the critical need to engage families in this formative assessment approach.

Placing children and families at the heart and as an essential aspect of Learning Stories can be further understood from a close examination of a California community college's collaborative approach.

Learning Stories in Practice at a Community College

> The parallel process of exploring Learning Stories not only allowed us to grow in our understanding of the pedagogy and philosophy of Learning Stories, but we heard each other's voices like we had never had before.
>
> — Jeannette Mulhern, Early Childhood Education Chair and Faculty, Cosumnes River College

According to Jeannette Mulhern, the Early Childhood Education Chair and Faculty at Cosumnes River College, the work that the Cosumnes River College Learning Story cohort did around Learning Stories in the last three years was nothing short of transformative. Jeannette shared that some preliminary work done by faculty paved the way for the implementation of Learning Stories within their Higher Education Early Childhood Education Department and Child Development Laboratory Center. There was a growing interest in the use of Learning Stories by faculty in their college coursework, which was fueled by senior faculty's introduction of the concept in 2013, following a New Zealand study tour.

The Cosumnes River College Learning Story inquiry group initially brought on Annie White as an outside expert to provide ongoing professional development on Learning Stories. One thing that was important to their inquiry group was that it was inclusive. Jeannette shared that they invited all Early Childhood Education faculty, Child Development staff (director, mentor teachers, interns, classroom assistants), and student peer educators to study together over the course of a year.

Together, they not only discussed how to create Learning Stories but also shared their work together and brainstormed ideas to address the realistic barriers and obstacles they may have faced for implementation. They developed processes, and in the end a core team whose members make up their inquiry group has continued to study together and revisit Learning Stories as a shared pedagogy. It was clear that Learning Stories strengthened the relationships between Early Childhood Education faculty, teachers at the Child Development Center, and Early Childhood Education students.

According to Jeannette, "The parallel process of exploring Learning Stories not only allowed us to grow in understanding the pedagogy and philosophy of Learning Stories, but we heard each other's voices like we had never had before." A deepening appreciation of what each other noticed and valued emerged. Jeannette shared that they began to recognize the "voice" of a Learning Story without having to be told who the author was, as "We now see each other as resources and benefit in leaning upon each other. We now know who to seek feedback [from] for editing and grammar or who helps us expand our thinking."

Jeannette explained how the group provides feedback and deepens the discussion.

> As a Learning Story inquiry group, we developed processes for feedback which work with our busy schedules and varying roles. We prefer to meet together and share our new or developing Learning Stories with each other. When this occurs, we make sure there is always tissue nearby as this is often a touching experience to celebrate our shared work together. We are excited to hear when a parent response is received after a Learning Story is shared and often cannot wait until our next scheduled meeting! We have often shared this information with each other over text message or "pop" into each other's classroom or office to share. And this is one of the unintended perks of Learning Stories, the connection that has been formed between the Learning Story cohort and the positive pedagogical and philosophy alignment that has resulted. It seems that we indirectly discuss pedagogy and philosophy of education regularly through our work with Learning Stories

Below are four Learning Stories written by the Cosumnes River College Early Childhood Education Department and Child Development Laboratory Center inquiry group members. Each Learning Story reflects the voices of teachers who share the context of their Learning Story practice that honors the voices of parents and families. These Learning Stories reflect the collaborative, strong collegial voices of this team who found the Learning Stories practice strengthened their relationships not only with families, but also with each other. The deep, caring relationships with parents, families, and children, and the extraordinary work they do as early educators' partners is passionately visible throughout their Learning Stories. The Cosumnes River College teaching community worked with children ranging from 2 to 18 years. The titles of the Learning Stories are

- "Gustavo's Rocks and Letters," by Vanesa Gutierrez
- "Leylanie's Family," by Eddie Tanimoto
- "My Dad Taught Me," by Lora Wardlaw
- "How Do I Get to the Ocean?" by Jeannette Mulhern

"Gustavo's Rocks and Letters" (Figure 6.4)

Why I Wrote the Learning Story . . .

> Gustavo started attending our program when he was only 3 years old and was learning English. Communicating with him in his home language, Spanish, helped me build a stronger relationship with him and his family. Gustavo would celebrate every new thing he accomplished and would be filled with joy by it. His signature celebration was raising his arms and shouting what he had done. At the time I wrote this Learning Story, Gustavo was starting to notice the letters of his name in the environment and looked for opportunities to create his name with different materials. When he saw the rocks on the table, he decided to use them to create the letter "G." He had accomplished creating the first letter of his name and celebrated by raising his arms and proclaiming, "My name!" Seeing the excitement in his face and his voice as it filled the room with joy, I instantly knew I had to write him a Learning Story to celebrate that special moment and share it with his family.
>
> Sharing the story with Gustavo's family was a delight. Monica, Gustavo's mom, shared with me about Gustavo's excitement for learning and finding the letters of his name everywhere he went. We both laughed as she shared with me about a time when Gustavo found the letter "G" at the hospital and excitedly shouted he had found his name, scaring the people around because of his resounding voice. Sharing the Learning Story with the family opened up more conversations about Gustavo's experiences at home and strengthened my relationship with his family even more. During a visit to Gustavo's house, his dad brought out the Learning Story for Gustavo to retell the moment as he remembered it, and dad read it to him again.

Gustavo's Rocks and Letters

Vanesa Gutierrez

I still remember the first few times you started to recognize the letters of your name and how enthusiastically you shared that with every person who was near you. Today, was not different. I could feel and see the joy you were experiencing about the letters you created.

Sincerely, Miss Vanesa

What It Means

Gustavo, your curiosity and sense of wonder have guided you to new discoveries. I have noticed how much you enjoy looking for opportunities that allow you to engage in finding, recognizing, and putting together the letters that make up your name. Today, you explored creating letters with rocks. You remembered how the letters that make up your name look like and were able to transfer that into writing.

You quickly found a chair, moved the rocks closer to you, along with a black board and a frame. I observed as you meticulously set up your workstation and began to place the rocks one by one on the board, creating the letter G. "My name!" you proclaimed, raising your arms, as the corner of your lips rose up from side to side in delight.

Your enthusiasm and interest for learning will continue to help you make new discoveries and tackle future challenges you may encounter in your education journey.

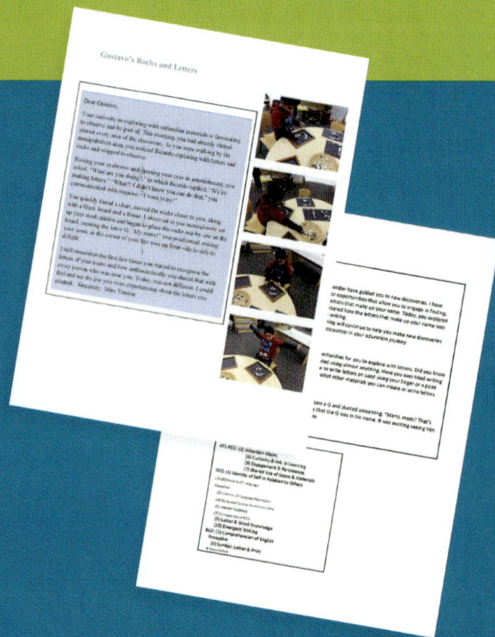

Opportunities and Possibilities

Gustavo, I will continue to provide opportunities for you to explore with letters. Did you know that letters and words can be represented using almost anything? Have you ever tried writing on sand? Perhaps, you can explore how to write letters on sand using your finger or a paint brush. Do you have any other ideas on what other materials you can create or write letters with?

Family's Response

We were at Mercy's Cafeteria, and he saw a G and started screaming, "Mami, mami! That's my name!" What he wanted to say was that the G was in his name. It was exciting seeing him excited. Everyone was laughing with him.

Figure 6.4 Original Learning Story "Gustavo's Rocks and Letters"

Sharing my Learning Story with my colleagues was extremely helpful because they helped me refine my ideas about the meaning of the story and suggested ways to continue to support Gustavo in the program. To truly honor Gustavo and his family, my colleagues suggested writing the story in their home language. Now, Gustavo has moved to the school-age classroom, and I feel his new teacher, who is in the Learning Story inquiry group, knows him much better because she learned more about him while we reflected together on this Learning Story a year ago.

— Vanesa Gutierrez, Teacher

"Leylanie's Family" (Figure 6.5)

Why I Wrote the Learning Story . . .

My Learning Story was initially written to Leylanie as a preschooler in our program. She was just receiving news that her mother was pregnant with her sister and she was going to be a big sister soon! This first story was a welcome back and helped not only introduce the concept of being a big sister, but helped build enthusiasm for Leylanie and develop curriculum and deepen connections within the classroom.

The current story was updated a year and a half later with an additional response from Leylanie's mother and me. We have still maintained contact as Leylanie has moved on to finishing kindergarten and is now a proud big sister. The response was written to acknowledge Leylanie for her accomplishments and express my appreciation for her and her family, not only in being promoted from kindergarten, but for being such an intelligent and sweet big sister. Due to the pandemic, Leylanie's program went virtual towards the end of the year, but fortunately because of this it also enabled myself to have the pleasure of attending her promotion party virtually and be there to support her in that way!

Sharing the story with the family has been my favorite part of the process. Before I had written the story, I did not know that Leylanie's mother was pregnant, so it opened up a wonderful new conversation and connection between us! Devon, Leylanie's mother, was so surprised and happy to hear and see Leylanie's growth since she started in our program and for her, this story was a good sign that Leylanie was definitely ready to be a big sister. With this strengthened connection we were able to maintain a connection as Leylanie left the program and even meet a few times. As the pandemic came and schools closed, the family was able to stay hopeful, expressing some possible concerns that they may have and how bummed they might feel if Leylanie doesn't get to participate as much in school experiences, but thankfully we were able to problem solve through most of these together and thus far things are still going great for the family!

Sharing the story with colleagues was a great joy for us all. Because it was Leylanie's first sibling I wanted to use this as a way for her to connect deeper to other children who may have some insight to offer and really help her understand what their perspectives are. This is where my colleagues came in. Not only were they able to share their expertise in books, handouts, and strategies for me to utilize with Leylanie and the family, but they were also able to help me identify children and families that would be great for Leylanie to connect with, which I utilized and included in the story as well. I have no doubt that these friendships and conversations throughout the year really helped prepare her to become the incredible big sister she is now!

— Eddie Tanimoto, Teacher

Leylanie's Family

Eddie Tanimoto

January 17, 2019

January 17, 2019
Leylanie's Family

Dear Leylanie,

It is so great to see you again after such a long winter break! I have really missed hearing all about you and your family and what you do every day! After a hug and kiss goodbye to your mom you immediately get ready to work. You crinkle your eyebrows, put your hand to your chin and say, "Mr. Eddie, everything is new in here, can we play?" I smiled, "Of course. We did move quite a few things around, a lot is new though, you are right. What do you think about the changes so far?" Without hesitation, you smiled, "I like it, now we can play blocks on this table, like this." You reached the nesting blocks and began setting them on the table. Naturally, you started to organize them by size and shape, but you surprised me when you separated them and said with a smile, "this big one is my dad, this one is my mom, this one is me and this little one is my sister. Or my brother. My mommy's pregnant, but we don't know if it's my brother or sister." You've always got so much to share! You continued to order the blocks and then you did something interesting. You reorganized the blocks: the biggest was on one side and next to it you placed the next size, and you moved the smallest of the blocks to fit right inside this one and lastly you fit the middle-sized block next to these two. Now all the blocks didn't fit together. You looked up and said, "it has to be this way. My sister is in my mommy's tummy, so it fits in like this. This even looks like her tummy now, see." I smiled and nodded, "you are right, it makes sense this way too." You continued to do the same with another set of nesting blocks and later reversed it back to the typical way. While putting the blocks away you said, "my sister won't be here for a while though, so I get to get ready for her and go to school a lot before she comes." I wonder how you learned all of this and were able to make such great connections.

As if this wasn't enough, you then reached inside and grabbed another set of blocks. This set was missing the smallest piece. Without batting an eye, you placed them in order. I paused and asked, "so is this big one dad, this middle one mom, and this little one you?" And of course, you smiled back, "No, silly. This big one is mom this time. This one is dad and this one is me. There's no little one here because it's still in my mom's tummy so she's bigger than dad right now." I couldn't help but smile, "Ooohhh that does make sense!" I replied, but on the inside, I was shouting, "how could she make this change so quickly?!?"

Figure 6.5 Original Learning Story "Leylanie's Family"

To which I quickly rationalized, well, it is Leylanie.

Our daily talks always make me feel so happy because you give me a little more insight each time on who you are . . . and that is one awesome individual!

Sincerely,

Mr. Eddie

What It Means

Leylanie, while working with the nesting blocks, not only were you able to place each block according to their size order, but you also gave the blocks identities that correlate with your family. Your dad being the largest and your soon to be born brother/sister as the smallest. During our talk you showed a great understanding of pregnancy and a great deal of excitement for being a big sister! Life and babies can be a little difficult to understand, but you have a strong understanding of how it all works. I am confident you will be a great big sister and a big help with your mom and dad!

From the first day I met you, you have always been kind, considerate and so thoughtful in everything you do and that continues to show to this day, especially when it comes to your future brother or sister. You always ask questions in a kind and mature way with this very calm and "Leylanie" way that lets others know you can handle a lot of information. When placing and identifying the blocks, you illustrated and narrated in this exact way. Very careful and exact in your placements and in how you went about identifying which family member would be represented.

Opportunities and Possibilities

More Important News . . .

Now that we all know you are going to be a big sister, we can start getting to know all the perks and responsibilities that come with it! Did you know there are a lot of books about becoming a big sister? I think you will find them very helpful because it can be a big change, but with a positive attitude you'll know all about it in no time! Our library has a lot of books just like this and I think if we ask Mr. Ben (Charlie's dad) he can even help us find them. Charlie also became a big brother recently, so maybe he can even give us some tips!

Additional Responses

Mom's Response: Leylanie, you are so beyond excited to finally be a big sister! It's something you wish on dandelions for when we go to the park. You are so helpful with planning for the new baby and helping me around the house. You are the smartest, sweetest little girl I have ever met, although I am a bit biased. I can't wait for your little sister to arrive and see the bond you share. I'm so grateful the new baby will have such a great role model like you to look up too. It's a true honor being your mother.

Leylanie's Response: I can't wait to be a big sister. I think I already am. When I say bye to mommy and kiss sister, I feel like I am. I even sometimes wish for her when I blow on my eyelashes like last time. You're in class right now mom? So, remember to have a great time, and I miss you. Love you. bye

June 26, 2020

Mr. Eddie: Leylanie, a little over a year has passed now, I can't believe that you have just completed your first year of Kindergarten! You've grown so much, you're reading, you know your presidents, your planets and it is so good to see you still love to play, jump, and have a great time everywhere you go! And of course, in typical Leylanie fashion, you are one of the greatest big sisters out there! Now that you both are older, I see you hold her and read to her and play with her all the time, even at your promotion party I could see how much you cared for her as you made sure she had her toys and took the time to make her laugh.

My Dad Taught Me (Anissa, age 11 years, 2 months)

Lora Wardlaw

Anissa, as you walked into the classroom you said hello and realized you were the first one to arrive. You put your things in your cubby and turned to scan the classroom. When you saw the materials on the table your eyes lit up like the sky on a Harvest moon evening. You gave me a look that said, can I? Remembering a conversation that you had with a classmate explaining your love for building things, it was no surprise when you wanted to do just that. I nodded, and you went right to work. You began by picking up pieces of what used to be a cart. Scratching your head with anxious curiosity about what it might be, you quickly tried piecing the random items of small wood pieces, ceramic wheels, screws and a wooden dowel together. As you handled the individual pieces your look of uncertainty became a look of clarity. You placed pieces back together until you were fairly certain it was back in its original form. You announced, "It's a cart of some kind." You asked if you could use Google to research your idea and sure enough you were right. Your knowledge of technology was obvious as you used the resource to not only find images of different kinds of carts but looked into the history of how they were used. You were pleased to see that carts were made in all different styles and the way you designed yours was similar to others you saw on the internet. You seemed happy with your plans to rebuild. Then as if I was talking to a professional design engineer you told me, "I am going to need some tools. I will make you a list." Your detailed list included a Philips screwdriver, screws, wood, a saw, and a measuring tape. I was impressed that you knew the difference between a Phillips and Standard screwdriver. Many adults do not know the difference. Your ability to plan ahead and predict the tools that you would need took me by surprise. I asked you how you knew so much about construction and you told me with an empowered voice, "My dad knows a lot about building things. Whenever we get a chance, we do things together". Your

Figure 6.6 Original Learning Story "My Dad Taught Me"

"My Dad Taught Me" (Figure 6.6)

Why I Wrote the Learning Story . . .

Throughout Anissa's five years at our center she had impressed upon me and the other children and adults in our classroom a warmth and kindness that seemed to radiate through all of us. She set examples and had the same expectations of others. In a community of diverse age groups, there is a complexity of understanding and compassion that each person attains as their daily lives together become intertwined.

Although at the time the story was written Anissa was 11 years old, her interactions with children 4–11 years of age helped to influence the learner she had become.

When I wrote this particular Learning Story to Anissa our Learning Story team met several times, as we often do when we are composing a story to a child. During our inquiry discussion, the team was familiar with Anissa and her family and gave positive and constructive criticism about the story. A colleague was intrigued about how close she seemed to her father and wanted to hear more about that in the story. Another

loving words about your dad brought back fond memories of me when I was a little girl watching my dad build things too. As you worked, one of your classmates asked if she could help you. You gave her opportunities to share her ideas and you said, "let's work together." You made her feel important as you told her, "I couldn't do this without you!" She held up each piece as you took apart the old pieces and prepared to measure and cut the replacement wood you needed. Using your Philips screwdriver, you replaced the axle with new wood and new screws and attached the old wheels. Pleased with your work you and your assistant gave each other a high five and beaming smile. You had recreated a new cart. Together you found the perfect spot, placed the finished cart in our outdoor garden and chose just the plant to go inside. You stood back and smiled as your classmates gathered to see what all the excitement was about. It made a beautiful addition to our garden.

Love, Miss Lora

What It Means

As you entered the room and began your work, I saw a confident, young lady sharing an idea and her workspace with her classmate. I heard you lifting up Fatima and working as a team. You considered Fatima's ideas while holding steadily on to your own. You used resources to check on your idea and confirm you were on the right track. I was there to support you and get you the tools you needed, but you seldom did. You showed problem solving skills and your knowledge of using real tools with safety in mind. Your words about your experiences with your father touched my heart. A father's influence in his daughter's life helps shape her self-esteem, self-image, and confidence. As you worked, I kept thinking what a successful young lady you will one day be. Then, I caught myself, you are that successful young lady.

Opportunities and Possibilities

Anissa, we have just a few short months together before you leave our center for middle school. I am wondering what I can offer you to support your love for building. Would you like to build more memories with your classmates? I will bring in different tools for you to examine and use. I have some electric drills and hand drills and additional loose parts you can explore. Let's invite your dad to come in and build a memory with us too.

Dad's Response

Anissa, seeing you hard at work and play really delights my heart. I love the way you use your mind to conceptualize something and execute it to make it come to life. That really impresses me. I believe you have the ability to do anything you would like to because you have the grit and tenacity to see it through. I'm proud of you daughter. When I looked at the picture of you building, I thought wow look at her go. It's my pleasure and joy to call you my daughter. Reach for the stars and beyond because I know you can catch some. Love, Daddy.

was interested in her ability to play and learn with such a diverse age group. Our inquiry group meetings are a time we gather and share our ideas. We feel comfortable and happy to hear from each other. We ask each other questions, and give positive feedback about the significance of the story. The way we are able to share at these meetings makes me a better writer and listener. In fact, I think, this team and these inquiry strategies make me a better teacher. When I read this Learning Story to Anissa, her face beamed with rays of happiness and delight. She took the story in her hand and stared at it for some time. After a few minutes, she looked up and asked, "Can I read this to my dad?" Her father often times hurried into the center picking up all the children and would rush to his next destination. Before he had the opportunity to repeat his daily pick-up routine, I gave him a call and asked if he could stay and talk a bit. This allowed him to be prepared for a longer pick-up. I remember that day so clearly. He sat at the table and Anissa read the story to him, his head hung down as he listened contently. A tear creeped down his cheek as she continued. When she finished, he pulled her close to him and told her, "You are my shining star." Before they left for home, I gave them the story, and Anissa said, "I'm going to keep it forever."

—Lora Wardlaw, Teacher

More Story Insights

The Learning Story "My Dad Taught Me" provides deeper understanding of the relationship between the father and child. This Learning Story offers insight into the values of the family, as the father responded, "I believe you have the ability to do anything you would like to do because you have the grit and tenacity to see it through." It is interesting to see the language of "grit and tenacity" being used by the father to affirm and validate the child as a competent and capable person. Learning Stories provide the opportunity for families to use these kinds of terms to describe their children in a public way that is very powerful, as it shapes the child's identity as a learner.

"How Do I Get to the Ocean?" (Figure 6.7)

Why I Wrote the Learning Story . . .

One of my roles as faculty is teaching the clinical practicum courses at Cosumnes River College. This means that I typically spend a significant amount of time in the Child Development Center, which is our early childhood education practicum laboratory on campus. Students have the opportunity to have these teachers mentor them in their preservice clinical experience with young children. Being in the lab school with children, college students, and mentor teachers is a part of my job that I value. I have the unique opportunity to get to know children and families as I work within the center classrooms.

Prior to meeting De'Von, I met his mother in my Introductory Early Childhood Education classroom. In that class I first introduced her to Learning Stories, not knowing that she and her son would be part of the campus lab school and receive numerous Learning Stories on her son.

When De'von was in the Blue Room [name of the classroom] preschool classroom he first called me "the teacher in the white room." He was referring to the silver doors that he passed daily where I taught college students. He later came to learn my first name, Jeannette, and would announce my arrival upon entering the classroom. I could have written many Learning Stories about De'Von as there were many moments worthy of attention. This Learning Story was written after I was captivated by De'Von's curiosity and the social nature of learning for De'Von. I was especially struck by the way that each adult that De'Von encountered along the way allowed him to own his own discovery of learning. It would have been so easy to answer his questions for him and end his discovery.

De'Von's mother and I reflected on the finished Learning Story together about his natural curiosity. Clearly, she had seen this same quality in her son as she had even purchased a shirt that said, "Never Lose Your Sense of Wonder." Over the years as De'Von has grown and moved through our classrooms his mother has shared her value on play and exploration for De'Von and her goal to keep him in the lab school's play-based program for as long as she can.

I wrote this Learning Story in a simple form so that it could be shared with my Introduction to Early Childhood Education course as a sample Learning Story. The class performs a live observation in the lab school on open-ended play and then creates a Learning Story based on that observation. Since that time, I have found that this more simple Learning Story has also helped support working teachers and clinical practice students to feel that regular use of Learning Stories is achievable.

—Jeannette Mulhern, Practicum Faculty

"How Do I Get to the Ocean?"

Jeannette Mulhern

What a joy it was to spend some time with you today De'von. As I entered the classroom you approached me holding a large conch shell and said, "Hmmm . . . How do I get to the Ocean? Hmmm . . ." I responded, "You are wondering how to get to the ocean?" To which you replied, "Yeah, it's in there and I can't get to it." You flipped over the conch shell and looked into the center where the shell curved into itself and pressed your fingers as far as you could. I then realized the meaning of your original question and asked, "How do you know where the ocean is?" Without saying a word, you placed the large conch shell up to my ear, gave a quiet pause, and said, "You hear it?" "Yes" I responded. Adding, "I do hear something that sounds like the ocean." You continued to ask your original question while trying to reach the center of the conch shell. I asked you if you had any ideas on how to get the ocean out and you sang to the conch shell employing the shell to bring you to the ocean. When that did not work, you danced with the shell continuing your song, "Ocean, ocean . . . please come out . . ." You then lead me to several teachers inside the classroom and in the yard whom you asked, "How do I get to the ocean?"

Jeannette Mulhern, Practicum Instructor

What It Means

De'von, you show an amazing curiosity, which is infectious. Today, watching you explore how to get to the ocean inside the conch shell, I realized that your exploration of the shell and sense of wonder led you on an adventure. You brought many people into your journey allowing them to be your companion in your discovery. This experience revealed your enthusiasm to creatively solve problems and learn more about your world. I hope that you always keep that ability to wonder and be curious about the world, bringing others along for the ride.

Opportunities and Possibilities

De'von, in order to expand on your curiosity of oceans and conch shells, I would provide additional discovery materials (magnifying glasses, various sizes of conch shells, and related books). I wonder if you have been to a beach. Perhaps we could look at photos of beaches and create our own ocean in the classroom. Another exploration we could explore is the how sound moves in different items. Would we hear the ocean in other items if we put them to our ear? I will continue to look for opportunities to nurture your curiosity and sense of wonder.

More Shell Engagement

De'von, I was so delighted when, a few days later, you brought me to the collection of conch shells in the science area. You explained, "Big, bigger, small." You lined the shells up in seriated order. I then realized that the shirt you had on said, "Never Lose Your Sense of Wonder". The statement on your shirt seemed to capture the value that your family has on this sense of wonder, which is evident in how you interact with the world. I hope you retain your awe and wonder as you grow.

Jeannette

Figure 6.7 Original Learning Story "How Do I Get to the Ocean?"

The teachers and faculty at Cosumnes River College Early Childhood Education Department and the Child Development Center Learning Story inquiry group members have shared their process of writing Learning Stories, how they shared with children, parents, families, college practicum students, and with each other. They report that Learning Stories have brought them closer as colleagues; they offer support through editing, reflecting, and inquiry, as Learning Stories have bridged their work to help create a united team, where the lab school teachers, college faculty, students, and families have become a closely knit family who listen deeply with respect for one another.

The Voice of the Children

The final Learning Story of this chapter provides opportunity and insight to reflect on a very different cultural context that prioritizes and honors the indigenous culture of Hawai'i. The teachers and faculty at Honolulu Community College in Hawai'i provide thoughtful family engagement that also honors the language and home culture of children and families. The Learning Story demonstrates a committed partnership between teachers, administrators, college faculty, and community. The commitment by each member to make visible and preserve the endangered language of the child is at the heart and a central focus of the story.

"A Flexible Builder" Written by Faculty at Honolulu Community College, Hawai'i

> The child's family is at the center of the Learning Story. — Janina (Nina) Martin, Assistant Professor, Lab School Director

Keiki Hau'oli Children Center is a Laboratory school serving the community college students. Teachers have been writing and using Learning Stories as the primary assessment for two years. The Learning Story written below is about Rhythm who is 3 years old and has been at the lab school since she was 3 months old. The teachers felt it very important to have her story translated and read in Hawaiian, Rhythm's home language. Her primary caregiver when she was in the infant room is the person who recorded the story in Hawaiian available in the QR code at the bottom of the Learning Story." When Rhythm was asked if it was okay to share this story for this book, she stated, "Yes! I want everyone to know how I'm learning!" (Figure 6.8).

In many ways, this Learning Story is an example of a collaborative effort since many community members contributed their knowledge and skills to make the story come alive. Lab faculty wrote the Learning Story to Rhythm. An instructor of the Hawaiian Language at the college translated the text, while the child's first primary caregiver made a recording reading the story in Hawaiian. Everyone contributed something so that Rhythm could hear her story in her home language, a language banned from use in schools up until 30 years ago. Below is an excerpt of an email from Rhythm's mom to Nina (Keao is Rhythm's Hawaiian name.):

Aloha e Nina,

". . . Mahalo nui loa again for letting us be a part of this opportunity. We shared about this with Keao and she actually gave verbal permission too. She was so excited for others to learn about how she's learning! Take good care and we hope to see you all soon!

Mahalo,
Jayleen, Keahi, and Keao"

More Story Insights

According to Rhythm's mom, the Learning Story in their native Hawaiian is a gift from the community to her child. The Learning Story "A Flexible Builder" demonstrates how families are able to contextualize their children's learning in school according to their particular family structures in history as well as their cultural orientations to supporting children within educational and community contexts. Perhaps, this could serve as a symbol of hope to highlight the value of all those small moments and languages that, unless preserved in a Learning Story such as this one, could be easily forgotten.

Ke Kūkulu 'Eleu

Written by Liz Hartline, Instructor; Supported by Janina Martin, Associate Professor and Lab Coordinator, Early Childhood Department; Translated by Hau'oli Lorenzo-Elarco, Hawaiian Studies faculty; Read by Pua'ena Viera, Infant Specialist at Honolulu Community College, Hawai'i (See in the QR code link below.)

Aloha mai e Rhythm,

Ho'omana'o anei 'oe i kāu hana 'ana ma ke pākaukau MagnaTiles? 'O ka mua, ua kūkulu 'oe i 'ale'o ki'eki'e me nā huinahā like. Akahele, akakūkulu, a ua aka'ohi'ohi 'oe i nā huinahā like, a ho'onohonoho kūpono 'ia a ki'eki'e akula nō. Ua 'ane hiki kona ki'eki'e i kou po'o! A laila, ke lawa kona ki'eki'e, ua ho'oholo 'oe e kūkulu a'e i hale huinākolu.

Ua 'ohi'ohi maila 'oe i nā mea e pono ai – 'o ke kahua nō ma mua. Ua ili mai nō ke kuleana kūkulu 'ale'o iā Kailani, a 'o ka 'ae akula nō ia ou me ka 'ōlelo "hiki nō!". He hui maika'i nō 'olua. Nāna nō ka 'ale'o huinahā like, a nāu ho'i ka hale huinakolu. 'O ke kahua ma mua, a laila, akapelu pū 'ia nō ho'okahi huinakolu nui, a pili pū nā mea a pau. Nui kāu pā'ani 'ana me ia mau huinakolu – ua 'ike akula wau i ka ma'a mau o kāu kūkulu like 'ana i ia 'ano hale.

A pau ihola nā hale 'elua i ke kūkulu 'ia – Na Kailani nō i kūkulu i ka 'ale'o ki'eki'e āu i ho'omaka ai, a nāu ho'i ka hale huinakolu. Piha ka na'au i ka ha'aheo ma muli o kāu hana nui me ka laulima o 'olua. 'Ōlelo akula 'oe, "ua kō e Kailani!" a pūliki ihola 'olua.

He nani nō ka 'ike maka 'ana iā 'oe e ho'okō pono ana i kāu mau 'i'ini, a me kāu hana kūpono a 'eleu ho'i me kāu hoa 'o Kailani.

He aha hou aku kā 'olua mea e kūkulu pū ai?

Me ke aloha, Anakē Lizzy

Nā mea e 'ike ai wau:

E Rhythm, maopopo loa nō ia'u kāu aloha nui i ka pā'ani 'ana me nā MagnaTiles – a he 'eleu nō ho'i kau! Hau'oli loa wau i ka 'ae koke 'ana iā Kailani, me ka 'ōlelo "hiki nō!", e komo pū i ka pā'ani i mea e kōkua aku ai iā 'oe ma ke kūkulu 'ana. He hō'ailona nō kēia no kou 'i'ini e hana like pū me kāu po'e hoa ma kekahi mea āu i ho'omaka ai. Eia kekahi, akāka loa nō kāu 'i'ini e hana pū me MagnaTiles – puni 'oe i ka pela 'ana i nā huinakolu me he kaupoku lā.

Nā 'ano ala e hele ai:

E Rhythm, i ki'i pēpē, i holoholona li'ili'i, a i 'elala paha na kou mau hale MagnaTile? 'O nā ka'a paha e komo ai i kekahi hale ka'a? Mali'a paha e ho'omau ana nō 'olua 'o Kailani i ke kūkulu 'ana i nā 'ale'o ki'eki'e A me nā kaupoku huinakolu? Mali'a paha, aia paha kekahi mau mea 'ē a'e e le'ale'a ai 'olua 'o Kailani me MagnaTiles?

To Listen to Ke Kūkulu 'Eleu, Scan Here:

To Listen to Nā mea e 'ike ai wau and Nā 'ano ala e hele ai, Scan Here:

Figure 6.8 Original Learning Story "A Flexible Builder"

A Flexible Builder

Dear Rhythm,

Do you remember when you were working at the magnaTiles table? First, you built a tall tower with squares. Carefully, carefully, you picked up the squares and placed them one by one as the tower got higher and higher. It was almost higher than your head. Then, after it got a little tall you decided to work on a triangle, structure.

You gathered what you needed—first the base. Kailani decided to take over your structure for you—and you said, "okay!" What a good team you guys made. She worked on this tower, while you worked on the triangle structure. First, you put the base together, then you carefully and slowly folded in the large triangles, at first one at a time, and then all together. You love working with these triangles. I've noticed you make these same structure, other times too.

Finally, both structures were finished—Kailani had to build the tall, tall square tower that you started, and you build your triangle structure. You were so proud of your hard work, and of your teamwork. You said, "we did a Kailani!" and you hugged your friend, so tight!

It was wonderful to see your focus on finishing why your mind, had decided to do, and to watch you be so flexible with your friend Kailani. I wonder what else you two will build together.

Love, Auntie Lizzie

What I Know Now

Rhythm, I now know how much you LOVE working with magnaTiles—and what a flexible player you can be. I was so impressed that when Kailani came over to help you, that you said, "okay!" when she started working on your building. This shows me that you are learning how to be comfortable with other friends, working on things you started. This also made me realize how much you've been working with triangle pieces. When you work with magnaTiles—you really love the way that they fall in together to make a roof.

Opportunities and Possibilities

Rhythm, I wonder if you would like to have the doll house dolls, small animals, or insects to make houses for with your magnaTiles structures? Or maybe cars to use them as garages? I wonder, if you and Kailani would like to work together to build big magnaTiles buildings that can have tall towers AND triangle roofs? I wonder if there are other ways for you to really have fun with both Kailani and magnaTiles?

Parent Response

Aloha mai e Keao,

With both you and māmā attending our own kula and learning all sorts of ʻike in different environments I don't always get to witness your adventurous feats and newfound findings. Thus, it's so amazing to hear all nā mo>olelo of your exciting adventures and your continuous exploration as you learn more about the honua around you, the people in your life, as well as yourself.

All your aunties and uncles at Keiki Hauʻoli Children's Center do such an amazing job supporting your curiosity and nurturing your love of learning. As if that wasn't enough they even go the extra mile and capture beautiful pictures, timeless moments, and your brave self taking on all sorts of feats, both big and small. When I am physically away from you the best parts of my day is when I receive photos of you simply being you. It makes a rough day so much smoother and a maikaʻi day more wonderful.

I love that you have a golden, genuine glow whenever you build, explore, learn, inquire, laugh, and smile. I hope that glow never dims, but gets brighter and brighter with each rich experience you have. May you share that glow wherever you go and when times seem a little darker than usual may it illuminate the way and help guide you through that current situation.

You are such a makana nani and I am so, so thankful Ke Akua chose me to be your mother. E ʻolu ʻolu ʻoe know that I need you just as much as you need me and I learn just as much from you as you do from me. An ʻōlelo noʻeau Papa Jay would always share with me and in fact, still does, is, *ʻAʻohe pau ka ʻike i ka hālau hoʻokahi*. This directly translates as "all knowledge is not learned in just one school," meaning that one can learn from many sources. And my dear . . . you are so blessed with so many, wide-ranged, irreplaceable sources you can learn from. Always remember that you are abundantly loved and deeply appreciated. I am incredibly proud of you and look forward to this beautiful gift of life we have together. Aloha nui loa wau iā ʻoe, with all my heart kuʻu kaikamahine.

Me ke aloha nui,
māmā

Figure 6.8 Original Learning Story "A Flexible Builder"

Chapter Summary

This chapter provided multiple examples of child, parent, family, community, and teacher voices. Each Learning Story makes visible and symbolizes a valued contributing member of a tightly woven together community, a community of learners. Learning Stories provide a way to show deep care and respect, honoring the diverse languages, cultures, and values of each other. As Nina eloquently stated above, the child and the family must be at the center of the Learning Story. They are at the heart of what matters most and what brings everyone to this important work together.

We started this chapter advocating for the importance of including parent voices and perspectives in child assessment practices. The Learning Stories showcased above, and throughout this book, demonstrate how educators' practice of writing and sharing Learning Stories deepens connections to and relationships with children, families, and each other. Learning Stories provide an innovative pathway to help to reclaim individual and collective voices in early childhood education. Too many current assessment methods in both public and private educational settings in the United States exclude families' contributions and children's learning outside classroom settings. It is vital that the field of early education and care policy and practice not allow data-driven assessment practices to continue to silence the voices and contributions of children, parents, and families. Instead, we urge you to consider assessment practices, such as Learning Stories, that make visible the voices of the diverse communities you serve, and of yourselves and fellow educators. Committing to engage and deeply think about Learning Stories practice through inquiry group work elevates and makes visible your values, care, and love for children, families, and this profession.

As you lift others, you lift yourself. You restore the joy of teaching through writing narrative stories that show your children as citizens with rights, as teachers with rights, entitled to social and educational justice (Souto-Manning 2016). These rights include ample time to reflect, dialogue, and implement meaningful assessment methods that show the authentic learning of children, and of teachers as learners, too.

Key Points

- Writing Learning Stories is a powerful and transformative experience for the teacher as observer, documenter, and storyteller.
- Sharing the stories and collaborating with parents can reshape and transform relationships between teachers and families, improving the overall socio-emotional climate of the school.
- Including parent/guardian voices in a Learning Story reinforces their role as the primary educator of their child.
- Honoring child and family contributions, as co collaborators, strengthens a truly authentic assessment practice that uplifts and reaffirms the notion of children with curiosity, skills, and talents.
- Multiple perspectives, including the opinions of children and their families—and not only those of the teachers, offer a more objective view of the child as a competent holistic learner.

References

Carr, M., & W. Lee. 2019. *Learning Stories in Practice.* Thousand Oaks, CA: Sage.

Claro, S., D. Paunesku, & C.S. Dweck. 2016. "Growth Mindset Tempers the Effects of Poverty on Academic Achievement." *Proceedings of the National Academy of Sciences* 113 (31): 8664–8668.

Curtis, D., & M. Carter. 2017. *Learning Together with Young Children: A Curriculum Framework for Reflective Teachers.* 2nd ed. St. Paul, MN: Redleaf Press.

Hatherly, A. 2006. "The Stories We Share: Using Narrative Assessment to Build Communities of Literacy Participants in Early Childhood Centres." *Australasian Journal of Early Childhood* 31 (1): 27–34.

Higgins, A., & S. Cherrington. 2017. "What's the Story?: Exploring Parent–Teacher Communication through ePortfolios." *Australasian Journal of Early Childhood* 42 (4): 13–21.

Remen, R.N. 1996. *Kitchen Table Wisdom: Stories that Heal.* Sydney, Australia: Pan Macmillan Australia.

Southcott, L.H. 2015. "Learning Stories: Connecting Parents, Celebrating Success, and Valuing Children's Theories." *Voices of Practitioners* 10: 34–50.

Souto-Manning, M. 2016. "Honoring and Building on the Rich Literacy Practices of Young Bilingual and Multilingual Learners." *The Reading Teacher* 70 (3): 263–271.

APPENDIX

Learning Stories Can Supplement Various Assessment Tools

Learning Stories can supplement aspects of an array of assessment tools commonly employed in early childhood education settings such as QRIS, CLASS, DRDP, ERS, ASQ, and PALS. These assessments are routinely used in federally and state funded early childhood settings to rate programs, social-emotional classroom atmosphere, classroom physical environments, and children's knowledge, developmental milestones, and phonological awareness, all in an effort to identify accountability and quality of services provided. Many of these tools were mentioned throughout this book in examples alongside Learning Stories; here we will provide brief descriptions of each.

Quality Rating and Improvement Systems (QRIS)

Quality rating and improvement systems, or QRIS, "assess, improve, and communicate the level of quality in early care and education settings"(Mitchell 2005). These state systems can be designed for use by all types of early childhood programs—child care centers, family child care homes, Head Start programs, and school-based preschool programs (Build Initiative, n.d.). States can make participation entirely voluntary, or they can make participation mandatory for certain providers, such as those that accept public funding or all programs that are licensed to operate in the state. QRIS offer a framework to

- Increase the availability of high-quality programs
- Deliver ongoing professional development and quality improvement supports to providers
- Strengthen parent understanding of program quality and the importance of high-quality child care and preschool

The QRIS rating takes approximately 60–90 minutes to complete (90–180 minutes for large sites) in which the rater will review documents related to children's health, vision, and hearing. In regards to assessments, the QRIS rater will review the ASQ and will also review child portfolios to verify child observations, work samples, and related DRDP-r 2015 documents if available. The rater will review the site's most recent ERS scores and the CLASS observations score if available. In centers, the rater will review classroom adult child ratios and group size as mandated by the state. At the end of the QRIS visit the rater shares the scores, which may be between 1 and 5, with high being the highest rating (First5 California).

Classroom Assessment Scoring System (CLASS)

The Classroom Assessment Scoring System (CLASS) is an observational instrument developed at the Curry School Center for Advanced Study of Teaching and Learning to assess classroom quality in PK–12 classrooms. CLASS began as part of a national study in early childhood development. Eventually, that research grew in significance as education policies shifted focus to teacher accountability and as a way for teachers to see how to see how their methods were working in the classroom (CASTL, n.d.). The CLASS instrument became a tool that could both measure teacher–student interactions in a classroom setting and offer resources for strengthening those interactions across any subject area or age group. CLASS is an observational teacher assessment tool that captures teacher behaviors linked to student gains. It includes four cycles of 15-minute observations of teachers and students by a certified CLASS observer. CLASS

› Provides programs, schools, and districts with reliable, valid data on teacher effectiveness.

› Creates a common language about effective teaching practices across subject areas and grade levels.

› Helps teachers better understand how their interactions in the classroom affect student learning.

› Documents improvements in the effectiveness of teachers' interactions with students.

Desired Results Developmental Profile (DRDP)

The California Department of Education's Early Education and Support Division Desired Results (DR) system is designed to improve the quality of programs and services provided to all children, birth through 12 years of age, who are enrolled in early care and education programs, and before- and after-school programs, and their families (CDE, n.d.). The assessment results are intended to be used by the teacher to plan curriculum for individual children and groups of children and to guide continuous program improvement. The DRDP-2015 is based on the previous DRDP instruments. It includes refinements made over the past several years and new elements that are essential to quality early childhood education. The Preschool Fundamental View DRDP-2015 is made up of eight domains and 43 measures (Desired Results Access Project, n.d.):

1. Approaches to learning–self regulation
2. Social and emotional development
3. Language and literacy development
4. English language development
5. Math and science
6. Physical development–health
7. History and social science
8. Visual and performing arts

The focus of each domain is on the acquisition of knowledge, skills, or behaviors that reflect each domain's developmental constructs.

Environment Rating Scales (ERS)

The Environment Rating Scales (ERS) is designed to assess overall program quality in a variety of early childhood and after-school settings, measuring both essential environmental provisions plus teacher-child interactions that affect the broad developmental needs of young children (FPG Child Development Institute, n.d.). Based on extensive research and field testing, the ERS tools have established interrater reliability and validity, making them especially useful for research and program evaluation, in addition to professional development and program improvement initiatives. The ERS are widely used for: state- and district-wide QRIS, continuous quality improvement, RTT-ELC funded programs, universal pre-K systems, culturally diverse and inclusive programs, teaching staff self-evaluation, professional development and coaching, and early childhood education courses. Suitable for use in inclusive and culturally diverse programs, ERS subscales and items evaluate

- Teacher-Child Interaction
- Health and Safety
- Physical Environment
- Curriculum
- Schedule and Program Structure

Ages and Stages Questionnaires (ASQ)

The Ages and Stages Questionnaires are designed to fit in with early childhood routines and engage parents (Ages and Stages, n.d.). The ASQ screeners are sets of age-appropriate questionnaires that are filled out by parents. There are two screeners in the ASQ system: ASQ-3, which looks at key areas of early development, and ASQ-SE2, which focuses on social-emotional development. ASQ-3 is a set of simple questionnaires to check child development. There are 21 ASQ-3 questionnaires for use with children from 1 month to 5½ years old (one questionnaire for each age range), plus an "Overall" section that asks open-ended questions about the child's development and lets parents weigh in with any concerns they may have. The five important areas of development that each questionnaire looks at are the following:

1. **Communication:** The child's language skills, both what the child understands and what he or she can say.
2. **Gross Motor:** How the child uses their arms and legs and other large muscles for sitting, crawling, walking, running, and other activities.
3. **Fine Motor:** The child's hand and finger movement and coordination.
4. **Problem Solving:** How the child plays with toys and solves problems.
5. **Personal-Social:** The child's self-help skills and interactions with others.

Phonological Awareness and Literacy Screening (PALS)

PALS-PreK is a phonological awareness and literacy screening that measures preschoolers' developing knowledge of important literacy fundamentals and offers guidance to teachers for tailoring instruction to children's specific needs (PALS Resource Center, n.d.). The assessment reflects skills that are predictive of future reading success and measures name writing ability, upper-case and lower-case alphabet recognition, letter sound and beginning sound production, print and word awareness, rhyme awareness, and nursery rhyme awareness. The assessment is designed to be administered to 4-year-old children in the fall of PreK in order to guide instruction during the year. A second administration in the spring of PreK serves to evaluate progress. The best interpretation of PALS-PreK results includes using child-level results to help meet children's specific needs and classroom-level results to guide instruction for the whole group. Scores from an entire classroom can inform teachers' curriculum planning so that they can provide and enhance opportunities for exploration and language-based literacy instruction for all children.

References

Ages and Stages. n.d. “Ages and Stages.” Baltimore: Brookes. Accessed January 4, 2021. www.agesandstages.com.

Build Initiative. n.d. “Quality Rating and Improvement Systems (QRIS).” Accessed January 4, 2021. www.buildinitiative.org/The-Issues/Early-Learning/Quality-QRIS.

CASTL (Center for Advanced Study of Teaching and Learning). n.d. “Classroom Assessment Scoring System.” Curry School of Education and Human Development, University of Virginia. Accessed January 4, 2021. https://curry.virginia.edu/classroom-assessment-scoring-system.

CDE (California Department of Education). 2019. “Introduction to Desired Results.” www.cde.ca.gov/sp/cd/ci/desiredresults.asp.

Desired Results Access Project. n.d. “Desired Results Access Project.” Napa County Office of Education, Research and Professional Development Center, California Department of Education. Accessed January 4, 2021. www.draccess.org.

First Five California (2017). State of California. Retrieved on April, 7, 2021. https://www.ccfc.ca.gov/

FPG (Franklin Porter Graham) Child Development Institute. n.d. “Environment Rating Scales.” University of North Carolina at Chapel Hill. Accessed January 4, 2021. https://ers.fpg.unc.edu.

PALS Resource Center. n.d. “PALS-PreK.” Accessed January 4, 2021. https://palsresource.info/pals-prek.

APPENDIX

B

Resources and Approaches for Starting Your Own Inquiry Group

Our book has described a number of different ways to conceptualize, implement, and facilitate inquiry groups in early childhood education. As we have discussed, inquiry groups can be created within one site or across sites to include a range of educators. The suggested activities in the online study guide (NAEYC.org/learning-stories) provide examples of both of these possibilities for working within an inquiry group. More information about these approaches can be found through the following resources and references.

Professional Associations and Projects

SALSA

www.salsa-global.org

www.salsa-global.org/resources

Supporting the Advancement of Learning Stories in America (SALSA) is an organization that provides resources for learning more about Learning Stories, including annual conferences, newsletters, access to webinars, and networking with those who are interested in Learning Stories in the United States. Isauro M. Escamilla and Annie White are founding members of SALSA and continue to play pivotal roles in the organization's outreach. The SALSA website also features a number of books on Learning Stories both from US and New Zealand educators, and links to Educa, an educational company promoting Learning Stories in the United States.

Educational Leadership Project

www.elp.co.nz

The Educational Leadership Project (Ltd) is an independent professional learning provider established in 2000 in New Zealand. Director Wendy Lee and the facilitator team inspire all those working with and alongside young children to strengthen their knowledge, understanding, and skills to make a difference in children's learning lives. Their website has sample Learning Stories for multiple ages.

Harvard University's Project Zero

https://pz.harvard.edu/resources/*see-think-wonder*

Harvard University's Project Zero is a pioneering research and development center focusing on multiple intelligences, languages, mathematics, creativity and the arts, and children's play.

The Zooms process (see below in the Schools section) utilizes teacher inquiry meetings via the use of a meeting protocol from Project Zero's "See, Think, Wonder" and the Ladder of Feedback.

Making Learning Visible, is a book co-written by Project Zero and Reggio Emilia that describes the processes of documentation and inquiry for children and teachers:

Project Zero & Reggio Children. 2001. *Making Learning Visible: Children as Individual and Group Learners.* Cambridge, MA: Reggio Children & Project Zero.

Educational Approaches

The Reggio Emilia Approach

Edwards, C., L. Gandini, & G. Forman. 2012. *The Hundred Languages of Children: The Reggio Emilia Experience in Transformation*, 3rd ed. Santa Barbara, CA: Praeger.

Edwards, C., & C. Rinaldi, eds. 2009. *The Diary of Laura: Perspectives on a Reggio Emilia Diary.* St. Paul, MN: Redleaf Press.

The early childhood schools in Reggio Emilia in Northern Italy, have garnered unprecedented international interest for their cohesive social and intellectual philosophy of teacher learning and development emphasizing inquiry, documentation, and collaboration (Edwards, Gandini, & Forman 2012). The Reggio educators have refined their approach over the last 40 years, tinkering with their key philosophical and pedagogical ideas on transforming the image of the child, and a social commitment to intellectual discourse and reflective practice. The Reggio approach to documentation involves the process of observing and recording children's learning experiences through different media with the goal of making children's learning visible to self, school, and community. The approach advocates for the process of inquiry, documentation, and reflection to be embedded in the daily lives of children and teachers and families. Documentation and inquiry happen daily, and there is ample time for professional dialogue and collaboration through educators' conversations and problem-solving together.

Critical Friends Group Approach

Kuh, L.P. 2012. "Promoting Communities of Practice and Parallel Process in Early Childhood Settings." *Journal of Early Childhood Teacher Education* 33 (1): 19–37.

The co-inquiry model has strong similarities with the Critical Friends Group approach as both make use of meeting protocols to ensure equitable participation for teachers and to support teachers' examination of and reflection on children's learning as well as next steps for instruction. The Critical Friends Group approach uses a variety of protocols such as the consultancy protocol, which involves specific roles and steps for the facilitator, presenter, and participants during an approximately 50-minute session. This approach has been practiced at a number of early childhood sites such as the Child Study and Development Center at the University of New Hampshire.

Early Childhood Consortium

The Early Childhood Consortium, originally started by Lisa Kuh, Debbie Lee Keenan, and Heidi Given in the Boston area, continues to serve a group of local early childhood educators as an ongoing forum for early childhood teacher inquiry and reflection. The Consortium meets six times a year in the Boston metro area and over the last seven years has included early childhood educators from private and public schools, family childcare settings, and from higher education. The group maintains an active public Facebook page (www.facebook.com/EarlychildhoodCFG) as well as a listserv.

Lead by Learning

https://weleadbylearning.org

www.facebook.com/weleadbylearning

Mills College in Oakland, California, houses Lead by Learning (formerly the Mills College Teacher Scholars), an organization that works with local schools on promoting inquiry, documentation, and reflection. Principals and teams of teachers are involved in documentation and dialogue around student learning. Lead by Learning uses certain protocols for organizing the inquiry group meetings between teachers and emphasizes the regular collection of data and materials on student learning in progress. The teacher inquirers can post their project findings and reflections online on the group's Facebook page, as well as presenting at yearly conferences of the organization. While the network has primarily focused on K–12 educators, it has a component for early childhood educators, and has especially focused on special education in early childhood education.

Schools

Eliot-Pearson Children's School: The Zooms Approach

https://sites.tufts.edu/eliotpearsonchildrensschool

Mardell, B., D. LeeKeenan, H. Given, D. Robinson, B. Merino, & Y. Liu-Constant. 2009. "Zooms: Promoting School-Wide Inquiry and Practice." *Voices of Practitioners* 4 (1): 1–15. https://pz.harvard.edu/sites/default/files/Voices_Zooms.pdf.

Zooms is a whole-school approach that utilizes documentation to promote teacher collaboration and dialogue. First pioneered in the early 2000s at the Eliot-Pearson Children's School at Tufts University in Medford, Massachusetts, Zooms links the tools for teacher inquiry with children's engagement in activities and projects. Founded upon the foundational Reggio ideas of a pedagogy of listening and visible learning, the centerpiece of the Zooms approach is documentation and the creation of documentation panels.

Helen Gordon Child Development Center at Portland State University

www.pdx.edu/helen-gordon-center

The Helen Gordon Child Development Center at Portland State University, started in the late 1970s, integrates elements of teacher inquiry, reflection, collaboration, and documentation. The school utilizes the Reggio approach of a studio (atelier) and studio teacher (atelierista) to promote aesthetic experiences for children that are then documented, displayed, and examined as part of the ongoing reflective life of the school. As it is a campus-based infant-toddler center and preschool, the teachers there work in concert with university-based researchers, adding another layer of teacher reflection and inquiry.

Boulder Journey School

https://boulderjourneyschool.com

The Boulder Journey School in Colorado is an independent school serving 200 children aged 0–5 that features a Reggio-inspired curriculum and school-wide inquiry focusing on children's explorations of their social and physical environment. Professional development at the school supports this inquiry work and emphasizes the identification of provocations for learning, eliciting questions from learners, and the selection of tools and materials to promote exploration and experimentation.

Joyce M. Huggins Early Education at Fresno State University: Co-Inquiry Model

http://fresnostate.edu/kremen/about/centers-projects/huggins/index.html

Abramson S. 2006. "Documentation - Communication - Action: Co-Inquiry Meetings for Facilitated Interchange." *Co-Inquiry Journal* 1 (1): 1–14.

Abramson, S. 2008. "Co-Inquiry: Documentation, Communication, Action." *Voices of Practitioners* 3 (2): 1–10.

The co-inquiry model in early childhood, as practiced at the Joyce M. Huggins Early Education at Fresno State University in California, utilizes a group protocol that emphasizes the three stages of documentation, communication, and action, and seeks to promote an egalitarian process for educators' participation and dialogue (Abramson 2006, 2008). The co-inquiry model also relies on a facilitator, often a veteran teacher, administrator, or outside expert in the field.

Hilltop Children's Center

https://hilltopcc.com/about-hilltop

Hilltop Children's Center is an internationally recognized school and professional development institute of early learning in Seattle, Washington. Hilltop has been providing and promoting child-centered early education for children aged 2–10 for over 40 years. Drawing inspiration from the schools of Reggio Emilia, Italy, Hilltop's faculty engages daily in rigorous reflective practice, collaboratively designing curriculum and environment around the emerging interests and curiosities of children. Hilltop is first and foremost a center of inquiry—for children, families, faculty, and the field. Hilltop educators "celebrate the wonders of childhood alongside children, while also deepening their teaching practice with children through regular reflection and study."

Books

Learning Stories in Practice

(Carr, M., & W. Lee. 2019. Thousand Oaks, CA: Sage)

This book, written by two of the most influential proponents of Learning Stories from New Zealand, contains nine chapters that focus on topics ranging from recognizing powerful frameworks to sharing responsibility with learners to the Learning Story Workshop. The book also features a large and varied collection of Learning Stories.

Learning Stories: Constructing Learner Identities in Early Education

(Carr, M., & W. Lee. 2012. Thousand Oaks, CA: Sage)

This book features seven chapters that focus on learner identities, role of story, agency and dialogue, connections across boundaries, recognizing learning continuities, appropriating knowledges and learning dispositions, and reconceptualizing assessment. A number of Learning Stories are featured in the book.

Assessment in Early Childhood Settings: Learning Stories.

(Carr, M. 2001. Thousand Oaks, CA: Sage)

This book focuses on assessment and the role of Learning Stories in a range of assessment processes ranging from describing to documenting to deciding. The book also addresses the role of assessment in helping educators understand children's learning and promote development, and how to shift teachers' thinking about assessment.

Children's Lively Minds: Schema Theory Made Visible.

(Curtis, D., & N. Jaboneta. 2019. St. Paul, MN: Redleaf Press)

Children's Lively Minds is filled with stories about real children exploring schema, such as building and knocking down block towers, followed by reflection and questions about what children might be learning. Viewing these actions through the lens of schema theory, developed by Jean Piaget, can help educators understand what's really going on in children's brains when they display these repetitive behaviors.

The Art of Awareness: How Observation Can Transform Your Teaching.

(Curtis, D., & M. Carter. 2012. St. Paul, MN: Redleaf Press)

This book, written by influential US early childhood educators Deb Curtis and Margie Carter, features 13 chapters focusing on topics ranging from observing for children's perspectives to observing children in nature to observing children with their families. The authors argue that educators need a way of teaching that mirrors their vision for children.

Our Inquiry, Our Practice: Undertaking, Supporting, and Learning from Early Childhood Teacher Research(ers).

(Perry, G., B. Henderson, & D.R. Meier. 2012. Washington, DC: NAEYC)

This edited volume highlights how teachers engage in the systematic study of their own practice to answer questions they have about teaching and learning and their own effectiveness. The book explores and describes what teacher research in early childhood settings looks like, why it is important to the field of early childhood education, and how teacher educators can support it.

Nature Education in Early Childhood Education: Integrating Inquiry and Practice. 2nd ed.

(Meier, D.R., & S. Sisk-Hilton, eds. 2020. New York: Routledge)

This edited book links inquiry, documentation, and reflection with nature and environmental education in early childhood education. The chapters provide foundational theory and research, as well as examples of early childhood settings actively engaged in linking inquiry and nature education.

Documentation and Inquiry in the Early Childhood Classroom: Research Stories from Urban Centers and Schools

(Kroll, L.R., & D.R. Meier. 2017. New York: Routledge)

This edited book provides relevant theory and research on critical forms and functions of inquiry as linked with professional development and growth in early childhood education. The chapters describe specific schools and settings dedicated to practicing systematic research and inquiry by educators individually and working with colleagues in inquiry groups.

Websites

Tom Drummond Resources and Writings

https://tomdrummond.com/looking-closely-at-children/writing-learning-stories

Tom Drummond is an innovative educator in Seattle who has pioneered Learning Stories in the United States, and his website offers a range of ideas and strategies for getting started on creating Learning Stories. The site also includes links to relevant schools and approaches focused on documentation, reflection, and Learning Stories.

Voices of Practitioners

NAEYC.org/vop

NAEYC's *Voices of Practitioners* is a long-running periodical founded by Barbara Henderson, Daniel Meier, and Gail Perry that showcases the inquiry work of early childhood educators and teacher educators. Currently, *Voices of Practitioners* is included in NAEYC's *Young Children* periodical.

About the Authors

The authors of this book bring a long history of work with Learning Stories and collaborative inquiry, documentation, and reflection. We have worked for many years with young children, their families, and early childhood educators working with young children on authentic assessment and critical pedagogy. We have also collaborated for the last three years in an online group of early childhood educators working with educators on integrating Learning Stories in inquiry groups. This group, whose members work in varied early childhood settings in California, has met monthly to present Learning Stories and to provide feedback for group members to expand the use of Learning Stories as integrated with ongoing face-to-face and online inquiry groups. Two of our coauthors, Isauro M. Escamilla and Annie White, are founding members of Supporting the Advancement of Learning Stories in America (SALSA) www.salsa-global.org, a nonprofit professional organization dedicated to the advancement of Learning Stories in early childhood education. This organization features a newsletter and local, state, and national conferences.

Isauro M. Escamilla, MA, born and raised in Veracruz, Mexico, is a Spanish/English dual language preschool teacher at Las Americas Early Education School in the San Francisco Unified School District, and is also currently a candidate in the Educational Leadership program at San Francisco State University. He has worked for many years on cultivating inquiry, documentation, and reflection as the heart of his teaching, and has traveled to New Zealand on three study trips to learn more about Learning Stories. He is a founding member and current co-facilitator of the Las Americas inquiry group. Isauro has a Masters of Arts in Education, with a concentration in early childhood.

Linda R. Kroll, PhD, is professor emerita of education at the School of Education at Mills College, Oakland, CA. She was a preschool teacher and then an elementary school teacher of K–3 for 10 years. At Mills College, she was the director of the early childhood education master's program and taught courses in development and learning, research in early childhood and elementary school classrooms, documentation as inquiry and research, and literacy learning. Her research and work with teachers has focused on constructivism in education, self-study research practices in teacher education, and teacher education at the early childhood and elementary level. Linda is currently working with an independent preschool on the creation of Learning Stories and sharing this work in an inquiry group.

Daniel R. Meier, PhD, is professor of elementary education at San Francisco State University and teaches courses in reading/language arts, multilingual development, narrative inquiry and memoir, qualitative research, and international education. His research focuses on children's language and literacy learning, and teacher inquiry and reflection in US and international contexts. Daniel has recently worked as a literacy teacher in a public preschool classroom in the San Francisco Bay area, and has worked with Isauro M. Escamilla for many years as the co-facilitator of the Las Americas inquiry group, San Francisco Unified School District.

Annie White, EdD, is assistant professor in the Early Childhood Studies program at California State University Channel Islands. She teaches undergraduate early childhood courses on curriculum and assessments where Learning Stories are used as the primary assessment for student early childhood teachers. Annie has worked with Early Head Start, Head Start, and State Preschool in various roles, and has provided trainings and coaching for teachers and family child care home providers. She has participated on national and international study tours and traveled to New Zealand and participated on several study trips, including two Learning Stories intensive studies. Annie conducts research on Learning Stories and how it is used as a tool for family engagement and is currently leading two Learning Stories inquiry group in Ventura County, CA.

Index

Page numbers followed by b, f, and t indicate boxes, figures, and tables, respectively.

naeyc®

NAEYC Membership

Is for Everyone

Wherever you're from, wherever you are, wherever you want to be—we have a level right for you.

Visit **NAEYC.org/ membership** to join today.

Entry Level Membership $30
Your digitally based introduction

Standard Membership $69
Unparalleled content and benefits

Premium Membership $150
The best value, the ultimate NAEYC experience

Interested in purchasing memberships for your team of 50 or more? Contact us at **GroupMembership@NAEYC.org**, to learn more about the benefits of a group membership purchase.

Advancing equity is a journey. Get started today.

NAEYC.org/shop

Promoting equity in your classroom is within your reach, and these books and e-books will give you the tools you need.

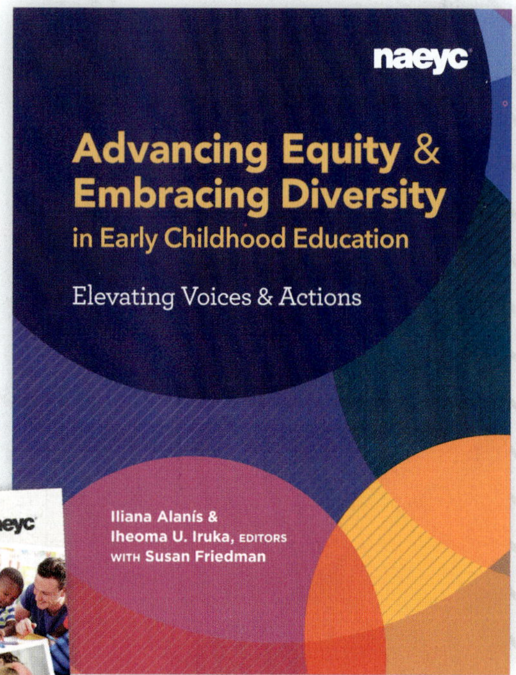

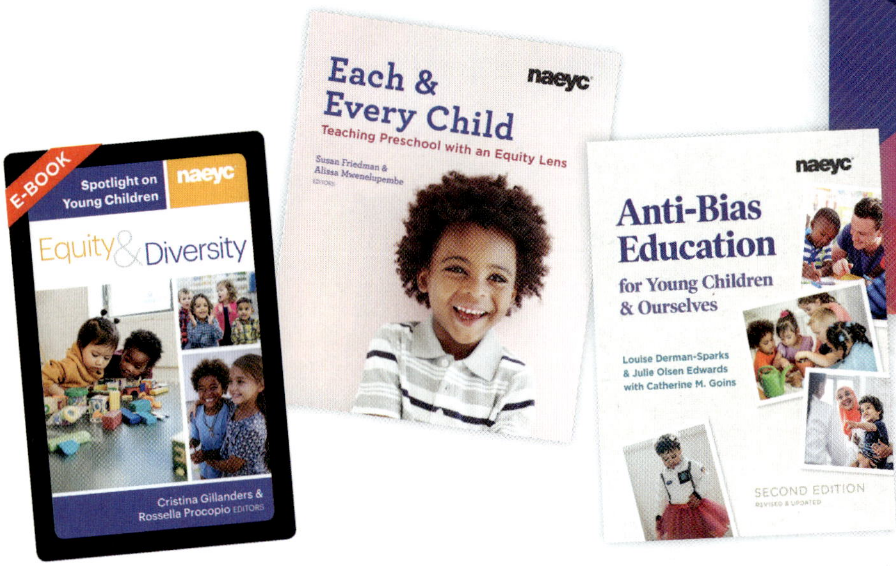

Plus, extend your learning online!

On-Demand Mini-Course
Each & Every Child: Teaching Preschool with an Equity Lens

On-Demand Module
Culturally Appropriate Positive Guidance

naeyc
National Association for the Education of Young Children

Buying for your team?
NAEYC books and online modules are ideal for your team trainings and workshops. Contact us today to learn about bulk purchase pricing.
202-350-8824 | marketsolutions@naeyc.org